Healing The Writer

A Personal Account of Overcoming PTSD

By Dan L. Hays

"Healing The Writer" by Dan L. Hays. ISBN 978-1-62137-726-9 (softcover) 978-1-62137-727-6 (eBook).

Published 2015 by Virtualbookworm.com Publishing Inc., P.O. Box 9949, College Station, TX 77842, US.

Manufactured in the United States of America.

Acknowledgements

I am very grateful for the insight of Karen McCarver, who prompted me to start on this manuscript when I would have postponed it, inspired this memoir with her intuition, and kept me on the path of the real story.

I really appreciate the support of Randi Fine, whose insight and guidance helped me clarify the true story in this book, and nudged me to let it go and complete it.

I was fortunate to have a lot of support to get through this story. Many thanks to Mary Nell Partin, David Nelson, Nick Degner, Carl Slater, Scott Bollig, Stash Serafin, Ellen Brown, Kerry Slavens, and Gil Namur, who kept me grounded and focused as I explored this story.

I deeply appreciate the contribution of Bob Kizer, who gave me not only the concept of inner child exercises, but valuable guidance during many rough spots.

I really appreciate the contributions of my editor Justine Goldberg, who gave me invaluable insights and direction when it was time to critique this sprawling memoir.

Thanks to the many people who have guided me along this healing journey, who have provided insight and guidance, and whose influence is evident in this manuscript.

I have changed a number of names in this work, to protect the anonymity of people where appropriate.

This book is dedicated to my Mother,
who has been a role model for my healing
journey.

Table of Contents

Part 5 - Freedom's Just Another Word

Part 6 - Moving To The Light

Prologue: What The Child Revealed

October 2003

H ere I was, a fifty-three-year-old man, about to do something to connect with his inner child. I had done healing exercises before, intended to access the wounded child within me, with a significant level of success. I felt a deep sense something was trying to come to the surface, and through the inner child it would be revealed. I stood in the middle of the library, the one place in the world where I felt safe, with my legal pad and pen in hand. I surveyed the floor for a secluded table. I spotted one in the back corner, where I would not be noticed or disturbed. I lay my legal pad and pen on the table and sat down.

The other times I did inner child work, it was a Gestalt, or empty chair, exercise. I would sit in one chair as the adult, and speak to the inner child. Then I would stand up, go and sit in the other chair, and answer as the child. But this time, since I was in a library, it felt right to do it as a written exercise.

I took a deep breath, quieted my mind, and allowed myself to relax. After a few minutes I felt ready to start, so I picked up the pen and began to write to my inner child, who I had named Little Danny Fear Child. As I wrote from the adult perspective, I sensed that the child answering was around eight years old, and I could visualize a frightened young child sitting in a corner. I was hoping to set him free, so we could let go of the Fear Child part.

"Danny. Are you ready to tell me what I can't see, about why I get locked up with my writing? You know – the thing the therapist said was really buried. Danny, it's time for me to write. Therefore I must let go of that old block. Can you understand that? You are safe now. I will take care of you. Letting go of this block will lead to great, great joy. Are you all right with all of this? If you are, just tell me – just blurt it out – no shame, no blame."

Danny spoke. "I was afraid if I wrote something, and someone read it, they might not like me because I said what I saw. People would know what was going on in our family. They would know our family was not all fine, and someone would get mad at me."

"What else? Go deeper – what's underneath that?"

"You really want to know?"

"Yes, I do. Please tell me."

"I always loved to read. I wanted to write stuff like that. I knew I would be good at it."

"Yes?"

"If I wrote a book and people read it, they might think I was weird or something, and not want to be around me. And I'd be lonely. I wouldn't be like all the other people who didn't write – and I'd be alone – again. I've been alone too much and I didn't want that. So I would not write."

"Why would you be alone?"

"Because writers are crazy – everybody knows that. And nobody wants to be around them."

"Who told you that?"

"Mamaw did."

"When?"

"When I went to visit her in Fort Worth. She asked me what I wanted to do when I grew up. I told her I wanted to write books. She said I didn't want to do that. Writers were crazy and people wouldn't want to be around me. They might have to put me away – lock me up somewhere. I didn't want that."

"Where were you when she told you that?"

"We were in her house."

"How did it feel when she said that?"

"I felt smothered by her always, but right then I felt killed."

"What did she look like when she said it?"

"She saw the look on my face, and she smiled. It was a cruel, 'I won' kind of smile."

"What did that feel like, seeing her face?"

"My stomach hurt, and I wanted to cry."

"Is there anything else?"

"Well, she kept saying it – all that week – until I wanted to go to Big Mommy's to get away. But I couldn't tell anyone about it."

"Why not?"

"Because Mamaw was a nurse, and she had heard it from Doctor Crowder, that creepy old guy she worked for. She said only those kind of people knew about stuff like this. She said don't tell anyone. They might think you were crazy just for asking and lock you up for that."

"Danny."

"Yes?"

"Do you understand that what she said was not true?"

"Kind of. Sort of."

"Remember what Mom said about writers one time?"

"Sort of."

"She said that writers were held in the highest regard. That they were revered in the world she grew up in – they were tremendously respected. Remember that?"

"Yes, I remember. But Mamaw was so sure. I didn't know what to believe."

"I understand. But it *was* true, and it *is* true. You will not be called crazy and get locked up if you are a famous writer. You will be honored, revered, and respected as a person who sees and speaks truth. That is the truth. We'll take all the time you need for you to get comfortable with that. Alright?"

"Yeah, OK. I like that. Will you remind me?"

"Of course I will. How are you feeling?"

"My stomach doesn't hurt so much."

"Why do you think that is?"

"Because I really, really want to write, and it made me very sad when I knew I wasn't supposed to."

"So you could write all along, but you thought you should not?"

"Oh yes, I could write any time I wanted to. I had fun with the stuff we wrote in junior high. But there was, you know, the crazy thing. So it was safer not to write, because I didn't want to get locked up."

"Danny, you just relax, and enjoy thinking about writing. You and I will release that old belief. So you can write freely and fully – with joy."

"I can do that. I am happy now."

Part One

Search For Peace

Chapter 1: Getting Words On Paper

I t was the summer of 1983, and I was living in Houston, Texas. I had met my good friend Barry at The Longhorn Café on Alabama Street for dinner. We liked eating there because they served great chicken-fried steak and mashed potatoes. Barry was one of the most multi-faceted people I'd ever been around. Though he was big, bearded, and looked like a mountain man, he was very well-read and extremely intelligent – he could speak knowledgeably about a wide range of subjects. He filled his time with a variety of interesting pursuits, like working as a river rafting guide on the weekends. He had just told me about his latest trip down the Guadalupe River, which sounded like a wild adventure. One raft tipped over and they had to rescue the occupants. He pushed away his now empty plate and asked, "So Dan, what have you been up to lately?"

I told him our men's softball team was doing really well this year, and that I was playing a lot of volleyball at the church on Sunday nights. I was helping our Sunday School class prepare for our fall retreat out at the Forest Glen church camp, and things were falling into place. Barry nodded in appreciation, because he and I had shared some enjoyable times sitting out by the campfire during those retreats. I thought for a moment, then said, "Oh, and I've finally been able to sit down and write more. I'm journaling most nights, and it feels good."

Barry's face broke out in a big smile, and he said, "That is awesome. I'm so glad to hear you say that. You know Dan; I've saved every letter you've ever written to me. When you become a famous author, I'm going to put them into a collection and call them *The Hays Chronicles*." I just sat back in stunned silence at the power of his words. "Your letters are amazing – it's like I'm listening to a philosopher or something – there is so much wisdom in what you say. I want to have a part in sharing the legacy of the Hays talent with the world." Barry's words hit me with incredible impact. But his words also touched a frustration that had nagged at me for many years.

When I was six years old I felt very connected with God. I had a sense of peace about my world, and knew – I just knew – that one day I would become a famous writer. It was a sense of destiny as tangible as anything I've ever experienced. "I am supposed to be a writer" was my truth. I started my first novel at age thirteen, something about a plot to overthrow the President. Then the movie *Seven Days In May* stole my story line, so I set the novel aside. When I was in the eighth grade, our class compiled a literary magazine. I published five poems and a short story, and once again was joyful about writing. Shortly after that, I stopped writing, and my joy for it was gone. I didn't know why.

By the time I was in college, it was difficult to write simple term papers, and to finish my master's thesis in graduate school was a tremendously difficult experience for me. I would have to sit for long periods of time to even write a short passage, even though I had done my research and knew what I wanted to say. I kept stopping, and there was a pain around writing that I did not understand.

I couldn't bring myself to say anything in response to Barry. It was too embarrassing to say I was stuck – unable to write creatively – and didn't know why.

———————

In 1980 I had started journaling, after not writing at all since I was a teenager. I needed an outlet to explore my thoughts and feelings. It didn't come easy. I would sit at a typewriter, or in front of a legal pad, *wanting* to write, knowing that I liked to write, *loved* to write, yet somehow feeling stuck. My attempts were tentative and halfhearted, and I had to force myself to make the effort. I was stymied, and felt a lot of pain about it.

I had heard the term writer's block, and when it happened to me I was physically unable to actually sit down and put words on paper. One night I sat down in my apartment to do some creative writing. I had run five miles that day, I was well-rested and felt relaxed, and it was time to try to write a story. I took out a legal pad and pen – writing longhand felt right. My cat Spenser watched me as he sat lazily on the couch. Suddenly I wasn't sure if I had set out the garbage for the next morning. I got up, took a bag of trash out to the curb, and set it down. I came back in the apartment, and my teeth felt gritty, so I went and brushed my teeth.

Ideas weren't coming to me for a story, so I walked around my apartment for a few minutes. I glanced up on the bookshelf at the row of self-help books, designed to allow a writer to break free creatively. I just rolled my eyes. I sat back down at my desk, and looked at the legal pad. Maybe I would write a story about somebody going somewhere. But where? That was the critical issue – I couldn't think of an idea about somebody going somewhere. Nothing was coming to me.

Suddenly I threw down the pen and yelled out in frustration, "Damn it! I want to write." Spenser opened his eyes at the noise, then settled back down and his eyes gradually closed. I envied how peaceful he looked, as I agonized over trying to write. Under the anger and frustration, I could feel a deep hurt and pain. Suddenly my throat closed up and I felt like crying. I felt a deep sense of loss down in my gut, but I didn't know why. I set the pen down, gave a last glance to the blank legal pad, and then turned on the TV.

The next day I wrote in my journal that I felt like an artist sitting before an easel, not knowing what he would paint. I didn't have any clue what I would write about – not even a vague idea. I had a deep desire to express myself in words, to peel away the different layers of life, and get at the essence of it. If I were an artist, a teacher might tell me to loosen up my strokes, that I was too stiff and rigid with my attempts to paint. Maybe I needed to just go with the flow and enjoy the writing process, and stop thinking about it so much. I just didn't know how to make that happen.

Recently I had read a book called *The Last Convertible* by Anton Myrer, and really appreciated his specific word choice and use of detail, which had led me through wonderful emotional experiences. God, how I wanted to be able to do that. I knew, I just knew, that I had powerful writing in me that was straining to be released. I had words in me that wanted to spill out on paper, but wouldn't. I could sympathize with the brush hovering over the canvas, unable to reach out and make that first stroke – I was terribly frustrated at not being able to actually write. Why was it such a struggle to put words on paper?

Chapter 2: To Find A Voice

T he participants of my Great Books study group had just finished a wonderful discussion, and were milling around the living room of the home where we met, rehashing the topic and visiting. My friend Joan pulled me off to one side and we sat on a couch to chat for a while. She said she was astonished by the depth and insight of my sharing, and was really impressed by my mastery in speaking. She wanted to talk with me about my writing. I could feel myself squirm a little. "Dan, you have a gift. You write very powerfully. It's time to let that gift loose." This was not the first time Joan had encouraged me to pursue my writing – it was just the most recent occasion.

Her words had a strong impact. Joan was an English teacher, very knowledgeable and intuitive, and I trusted her judgment completely. I had corresponded regularly with Joan when she lived out of town, and now she told me she had saved my letters. It was hard to discount what she was saying. But I tried.

"I hear you, Joan, but it's tough to find a place to start." I could hear the defeat in my voice. "I just don't know what to write about." I looked over at the puzzled look on

Joan's face. I could completely understand her confusion – I was confused too.

The drive to write was so strong I found myself trying to push through the writer's block. I had begun attending Adult Children of Alcoholics twelve-step meetings, specifically focused on people who had grown up with alcoholism. Those old experiences and emotions were bottled up inside me, needing an outlet, wanting to bubble forth and be released. I began to journal extensively about my experiences growing up, and how they affected me as an adult. I had found a way to explore topics that were much on my mind.

I struggled to find my voice. When I moved beyond free-flow journaling and tried to write on a specific topic, my words sounded wooden – like a toy soldier from the Nutcracker spoke them. How could I change that? There was a really odd thing, though – I had always been a very active letter writer, and wrote regularly to a lot of friends. Many of them, including Joan, had praised my writing skills. When I wrote letters, my words flowed freely and effortlessly. I was always puzzled when a friend raved about something I'd written – I just dashed letters off quickly, and they were easy to compose.

One day while writing a letter, I connected the dots and saw a new idea. Talk about your experiences and whatever is on your mind – only write it like a letter to a friend. It felt like a big awakening. I knew writing on a topic would have to be handwritten – like a letter. Something about the tactile experience of putting pen to paper had always been comfortable for me. I relaxed into the writing process that way, and thoughts just seemed to connect and flow.

I gave it a try. After all, I had nothing to lose.

Dear Joan,

As I look back at my past and what has happened, I'm struck by the feeling of searching I continually experienced. On ski trips, while scuba diving, going to parties, on a date; whatever the activity, there was always nagging at the back of my brain a vague uneasiness. There was some part of me saying, "This isn't it", some deep-seated need still unmet. It was a long time before I could even identify that the feeling was there. It felt like a void, a sense of emptiness, essential aloneness. I've been so lonely standing in a crowd, I ached. Even when I went skiing with good friends, in what I consider God's country, with the most beautiful scenery on earth, the little message still nagged, "This isn't it." What I was searching for was in one word - peace. I wanted to feel at peace with my world and myself. But what did the word peace really mean? It was just a term I'd heard a lot of people talk about.

My misconception was that peace came from external sources – from without. It didn't happen that way, and all I did was put tremendous strain on people and events to fill that need. In my experience, peace must come from within. I took a long time to get that message, yet the result was real and totally sufficient. Having peace within leads to joy, and joy was unexpected for me. I didn't think I'd ever see it and I didn't think I deserved it.

Those are just the first thoughts that come to mind – more later.

Dan

I had found my voice.

Chapter 3: The Commitment To Write

As I walked out of the Rice University Library, I ran into Lindsey, a casual acquaintance from our Sunday School class at church. "Hi Dan. What are you doing here?" she asked. I wasn't a student at the school, and had no real reason to be in the library. My friend looked really puzzled, and a bit alarmed at the panicked look on my face.

"Oh, I just wanted to look for some books that I couldn't find in the public library." I could hear how lame my answer sounded – I didn't have any books, just a legal pad and a copy of the *Writer's Market* under my arm.

Something about this brought up a deep fear – being discovered in the library, writing a book. My heart raced, and my breathing went very shallow. Why was it so scary to run into someone at the library? Did this have something to do with my struggle to write? Luckily, my friend let me off the hook by saying she had to leave. She looked disconcerted by my awkwardness, but waved goodbye and walked off with a wave. I breathed a deep sigh of relief, but it took me a few minutes to calm down. There was a rush of adrenalin shooting through me. My response didn't line up with what had just happened. I was hiding in the library to write a book, and didn't want anyone to know. Why was that important?

At last I could write my thoughts in journals, but I didn't let anyone know I was doing it. For the last four years, I would fill up a 120-page notebook about once a month with my thoughts and feelings. I kept writing in the "Dear Joan" format, because that voice had become very familiar. But those were very private, very random notes – I would just write whatever came to me, with no thought to theme or topic. I felt a tremendous relief in having that outlet.

Journaling was fine, but I now faced a dilemma. I had recently read a book called *A Bridge Across Forever*, in which the author, Richard Bach, had recounted taking a writing course in school. To get an A in the class a student had to bring the teacher proof that they had published something. It resonated with something I had felt for years – publication was the final step in releasing a book to the world, and it was my ultimate goal as a writer. Was I ready for that?

Early in 1985 I took a step of faith by making a formal commitment to writing. I set a goal to submit a manuscript to a publisher by the end of the year. I was so frustrated by my inability to put pen to paper that I was willing to try something different, to "prime the pump" and break beyond the writing block. With work projects, when the boss assigned me a task, I was very diligent and always completed the work, and usually turned it in early. By assigning myself a writing project, hopefully I could approach it with that same work ethic. I currently worked as a contract landman in the oil industry, and when my current job ended, I took time off to write.

An idea began to form and take shape for a story I wanted to share. I had recently read my journal notes from the previous several years, and was appalled to see my negative relating habits, how I clutched at and tried to control people. A theme started to emerge - something like "reach out and grab someone" – a study of how my clinging to people pushed them away.

I started driving daily to the Rice campus and laying out my writing materials on a table in the very back of the library. I wanted to be very businesslike with my writing, and set up a schedule to be there eight hours a day, five days a week, just like I would for my job. I knew I wouldn't write all the time, but that I'd spend a lot of the time reading journal notes and reflecting. I just wanted to be in position to capture words if the writing began to flow. Some days a few thoughts would connect, and I would jot some notes. Other days, nothing seemed to happen – but I was there just in case. I would get up and wander around the stacks of the library, letting thoughts come together and formulate into themes I wanted to explore.

The other reason – unstated – to work at the Rice library, was that no one could see me and know about my writing goal. I didn't see it as odd at the time, but rationalized that I didn't want to give regular updates on my writing process to everyone I knew. I had a wide circle of friends, and felt that constant questions about my progress would make me nervous. My stated reason had some validity, but there was more underneath which I couldn't see. Something else was making me want to keep my writing secret, but I couldn't put it into words. I didn't know what was making me do this, but it was terribly important at the time.

One day I sat at a desk, in the back of the stacks, looking at a legal pad, unable to think of anything to write. My legs started to shake, so I got up and walked around for a few minutes, to loosen them up. I sat back down and felt my heart race, like I was being chased. No thoughts came to mind, but I continued to sit and look at the legal pad, ready to capture any grain of inspiration. Most of the afternoon I just sat there, and finally after the leg shaking died down, I packed up and went home.

The next day things weren't as locked up, and I jotted down more notes on the theme which had emerged. I occasionally reviewed some of my journal entries. There was a clear half hour where the thoughts flowed and I wrote down what felt like some powerful and solid thoughts. I began to feel anxious, my legs started to shake and quiver again, and I had to walk around for a while. This went on day after day – there were some days where I would just sit at the desk. There were some days where it felt like thoughts floated in the back of my mind, but I couldn't bring them to the surface. I would sit for a while, to let random thoughts collect in a coherent order. At a certain point, when I began to write, the thoughts just flowed out in a logical and very natural order, and made a lot of sense.

After about two months I went back to review my notes, and realized I had told a story. I started to call the manuscript *Search For Happiness*, but later changed the title to *Search For Peace*, which was more accurate for the nature of my journey. It took a while to appreciate that I had completed my goal of writing a book. The thought made me really nervous, so it wasn't as satisfying as I had expected.

Around that same time I got back together with a woman who I had previously dated. Though we were both very skittish about renewing our relationship, we had some good experiences together. She was trying to find a house to rent, but couldn't afford what she wanted. I had what at the time seemed like a very good idea. She could rent the house she wanted, and I would rent a room from her to use as my writing office. (The codependency of this offer merits its own book – but that's another story altogether.)

There was a desk and writing area nicely set up in my garage apartment, and it was a comfortable place to write. But the experience of getting up and going to the library – to a separate place – every day, had made me realize it would be more productive to go somewhere besides my apartment to write. On one hand, it made a lot of sense at the time. In reality, it was a justification that allowed me to keep my writing hidden.

I moved my writing desk, file cabinet, and materials into a room at Sheila's and began to go over there to write. I took more time off work, and spent most of the summer cleaning up and editing *Search For Peace*. I also spent time at the Rice Library to research the publishing industry, to explore how to get a book published. There were also many hours of feeling a sort of disconnected fear, where my legs would shake, I'd feel tremendous anxiety, and couldn't calm down. I was hiding out in a place that no one knew about, not telling anyone what I was doing. Later I would understand, but at that moment, I was baffled by the need for all of this secrecy.

Chapter 4: Seeking Publication

O ne day I was able to say, "I did it. I wrote a book!" I was elated on one hand, but on the other, the statement made me very nervous. I had made a commitment to myself to submit a manuscript to a publisher before the end of 1985, and now it was time to finish the job.

I lay in bed wide awake late that night, really restless. I wouldn't fall asleep any time soon. My legs were shaking, like I wanted to run somewhere, get away, but I didn't know how to find safety. I wanted to jump out of my body, and wasn't sure what was going on. I had almost drifted asleep when a noise outside jolted me – like someone had pumped adrenalin directly into my veins. I was on high alert, and felt young, very young. I couldn't tell what was safe and what was not. I didn't know where this was coming from.

A couple of days later, I happened to glance at my journal and noticed something – I had written about working on my "first manuscript." It was astonishing that I had already declared my intention to write more than one book. It gave me a flare of sudden anxiety, and a serious need to get up and move around. There was nothing on my schedule, so I just drove around for a while until my breathing slowed down, and I was able to relax. I was awake late that night, and sleep just would not find me.

At the end of 1985 I was distracted, and found a lot of reasons not to think about books and publishers. I spent a lot of time just being busy – I was the jolly guest at church parties and holiday events, and managed to fill up my days by staying very active. That continued after the holidays, and by the end of January 1986, I decided that busy just wasn't going to get a letter in the mail to publishers. Something different needed to happen. I came up with an idea, and called a friend from the ACA program who knew I was writing a book. His name was Dave. Tall, lanky, and thin-faced, he had dark brown hair and was thoughtful and well-spoken. He was also one of the most gifted songwriters and guitar players that I had ever met. He sang with a bluesy, Southern voice, raspy from too many cigarettes, and I had been to a lot of venues to hear him perform. He and I had gotten to know each other pretty well, and I felt I could rely on him for what I had in mind.

"Hey Dave, how's it going?"

"Doing fine Dan, how are you doing?"

"I'm doing OK, but I need some help. I'm stuck – I can't bring myself to send my manuscript to publishers. I just can't seem to get it done."

"That must be tough – I know you've put a lot of work in on that."

"It really is – it's frustrating. Anyway, the reason I'm calling is I could sure use some help, and wonder if you'd be willing to give me a hand?"

"Absolutely, Dan, what do you need?"

"I need someone to keep me on track. I'm the one who is responsible for actually putting letters in the mail. But I want to know someone is going to follow up and make sure I get that done. Could you call me on February 28th, and ask me if I have submitted my book to twenty publishers? I'll do the work, and you don't have to make me do anything. If I know you're going to call and ask, I think I'll be able to get going on this."

"Of course, Dan, I'll be glad to do that. This is pretty amazing, actually. Truth be told, I'm jealous, but in a good sort of way. You're living out your dream, and that's really cool. You don't need anything else from me?"

"No, Dave. I think this might work. You know how responsible I am – if I commit to do this, it will motivate me to break through the fear."

I had always thought the term "paralyzed by fear" was just an expression, until late that night. It was like someone had frozen my body – I couldn't get up out of bed. I couldn't move or even roll over, except for the shaking that I couldn't do anything about. Now it was both my arms and my legs – my legs would shake for a while, and it would subside. Then my arms would shake. I was breathing like I was running too fast in a race, and couldn't slow down. I could feel my heart pumping. I didn't know what else to do, so I just lay there and let the shaking go freely until it finally subsided. I slept uneasily that night, and woke unrested. I had taken a "feelings" seminar that said if we let old stuck feelings release from our bodies it helped us be free of them. That wasn't much comfort as I was going through it.

Several days later at an ACA meeting, my friend Lou came up and asked me how the writing was going. I almost tried to push him – to get him away from me, until I caught myself. I mumbled, "It's going alright. The manuscript is almost finished."

"Don't forget what I told you Dan. I know a literary agent in New York, and have a publishing contact in Houston. If you want to talk with them, I could set it up."

I was shocked – I had no memory that he had ever told me that. I never asked him to follow up.

Several weeks later, I called Dave – three days early, to tell him he wouldn't need to call me on February 28th. I had dropped all of the query letters in the mail. I didn't mention the series of sleepless nights that had consumed most of my February, the constant legs and arms shaking, feeling on constant alert, terrified that something awful was about to happen, and how frightening I found the whole experience. He was a good friend, and would have listened to my fears. But talking about it might have made some bad thing happen, a tragedy that I could feel but could not name, so I said nothing.

A couple of days later, on a conscious level it was like the whole thing had never happened – like I hadn't just dropped letters to publishers in the mail. I had blocked from my mind that publishers were about to receive a letter from me to ask about publication. I was shocked when someone asked about my book. They reminded me of something my mind was trying hard to forget.

When I started to get responses – all rejections – I didn't even mention them in my journal. It hurt too much to acknowledge being rejected. Once the final rejection came in, I set it with the others and walked off without feeling anything.

Several months after I got the last rejection letter from the traditional publishers, I could finally talk about it. I told a friend about being rejected for publication. She had a surprising response.

"Dan, you don't really look that disappointed. You say you are, but somehow I'm sensing that it's not really that deep."

I sat with that for a moment, not really knowing what to say. I thought I was sad and disappointed – I'd been telling myself that. But was I really?

"Where did you send your manuscript?" she asked.

"I sent it to a whole list of publishers – most of the major ones that looked like they'd be interested."

"Did you send it to any of the recovery publishers? From the way your book sounds, I'd think that would be the real market for your book – those people would really benefit from it."

"No, I hadn't thought of that."

"So you're setting yourself up to fail."

Her words felt pretty harsh – she usually spoke her mind without varnish. I silently reflected on what she had said. Later that night, I had to agree that she made a lot of sense. My book would fit in perfectly with the spiritual journey of people in the recovery world. I felt some resistance – was part of it that I didn't want to admit she was right?

After a couple of days – where I could feel like I had made the idea my own – I made up a short list of recovery publishers to query about my manuscript. Since I had just gotten such a resounding rejection from the traditional publishers, I didn't get my hopes up, and kept my expectations very low.

Chapter 5: Fantastic News For A Writer

A ugust 1986.
"Mr. Hays, I spent all weekend reading *Search For Peace*, and I just couldn't put it down. I'd like to talk with you about publishing your book." Those were thrilling words for a writer to hear from a publisher. It was hard to breathe, and I was overcome with a wave of excitement. Soon enough, though, I would be overcome with a different feeling – terror.

———

The main resource being used at ACA twelve-step meetings I attended during that time was a book entitled *It Will Never Happen to Me*, by a therapist named Dr. Claudia Black. In the book she describes the effects of growing up in a family where alcoholism was present. At the suggestion of a friend, I contacted her publishing company, and on their recommendation sent a copy of *Search For Peace* to them, on Thursday, August 15th.

My phone rang early on the morning of Monday, August 19, 1986.

"Mr. Hays, my name is Jack Fahey and I represent Mac Publishing. I love your manuscript, and am very interested. I've read the first twenty-nine pages, and I plan to finish it this afternoon, and will give it to Claudia Black."

"Okay," I replied casually, as if this was an everyday occurrence. I was numb with shock – some part of me realizing that this was a big deal if he was calling me after only having the manuscript for a couple of days.

"My marketing strategy is very specialized," Fahey continued. "I'll publish within six months. The first year, I'll target the therapeutic community and treatment centers. I'll put the book in our catalogue, and take copies to all of Claudia's presentations. The second year I'll begin to focus on the bookstores and let demand pull it through. Claudia's book is coming up on four hundred thousand sales. We publish very selectively – only three books in 1986, three more scheduled for 1987."

Because of my business background, I started to evaluate as I listened. He proposed a very solid marketing strategy. It was difficult to breathe and I felt my pulse speed up. This was an incredible offer – to have the publisher call and describe a very aggressive marketing campaign for my book, targeted to the best market for my topic. I took a deep breath.

"As I said, I'm very excited, but I'm also impulsive," Fahey continued. "So I want to slow down a bit. I'd like for you to call me tomorrow morning and we'll talk it over. I'd also like to give you the number of a business associate there in Houston who can give you some perspective about me."

I still felt numb and overwhelmed by what I was hearing, but began to regain a bit of composure. I went into an automatic response, and my business voice took over. "Mr. Fahey," I said, "I like your style and marketing concept, and I like to go slow as well. I just want to let you know I've submitted the manuscript to several other recovery publishers."

"Good. It's always smart to check out several options. Like I said, call this gentleman who knows me, and let's talk again tomorrow."

I got off the phone and sat for a minute, trying to let the whole thing sink in. Dr. Claudia Black was considered one of the pioneers for the families of alcoholics movement. I hadn't found any books about growing up in an alcoholic family by a writer who went through it – the few I had been able to find on that topic were written by therapists. *Search For Peace* could be a new resource in a community that was growing and needed better support material. I had just been approached by one of the leaders in the industry, wanting to use all their reputation to promote and back my book.

My words would reach people like me, who had been as lost as I was when I walked into my first twelve-step meeting. The enormity of this shocked me. I would have been really grateful to find a similar book when I was struggling to shed light on those issues in my life. It would have given me great comfort to know I was not the only one suffering from those problems.

I called Fahey's contact, who told me that Jack was a "straight shooter, a very gifted and astute businessman, with lots of good marketing experience in the therapeutic community" – further confirmation of the power of what was being presented.

On Wednesday I called Jack Fahey back. He said he was still excited after finishing the book, and that anything he really got excited about was publishable. He excitedly praised some of its passages – he actually had the manuscript in his hand and was reading my own words to me. I was in awe of how powerfully the book had affected him. He said about 15 percent of the manuscript would need some work for the market he thought it would appeal to, especially the God part, because of my use of Bible references and talk about intimacy with God. He felt it might need a preface for God as I Understand Him, so not to scare off the twelve-step folks. I agreed with that, since I had written about the God part more from a church perspective. That might not be as comfortable for people in the twelve-step programs, who talked more about spirituality than religion, and were more open to alternative viewpoints of God than I had been exposed to in the church.

I agreed with the changes he was proposing and told him so.

Jack told me that their financial arrangement was to share fifteen percent of gross sales. A shorter book like mine would likely be published as an original paperback, and be priced at $3.95 or $4.95 per copy.

"Paperback is fine, Jack." I said. "That would be more affordable."

"Really?"

"Monetary reward isn't my primary objective. I'd rather get it to the people who need it."

"Dan, I like your style."

———

A publisher well established in the target market, an advocate who was excited and enthusiastic about my book, and also a solid businessman with a definite marketing plan. It was the opportunity every writer would love to experience.

Why was part of me shaking inside? It didn't feel like excitement – my stomach felt queasy, like when I would come home from school as a teenager, wondering what mood Dad would be in. I should have been really thrilled, but deep inside me there was a blackness, a dread that I was only partially aware of on a conscious level.

I had to explore this feeling of dread, and I suspected the answer lay in the past. I had a feeling somehow my dad was involved, but didn't know why I felt that way.

Chapter 6: Time To Publish a Book

B y October, it was apparent that I was not going to follow up with Jack Fahey about publishing *Search For Peace*. I knew it was a great opportunity, but I just couldn't bring myself to call him back. Part of me was sad, but part of me, down where I didn't want to admit it, was greatly relieved. I justified it by telling myself that I had lost the thread of the book, and needed to let it sit for a while, so I could return to the book later with a fresh perspective. Did it make much sense, especially with a publisher who was very interested? It really didn't, but I made myself accept it at the time.

I thought I knew why I was stopping short. It was because of the poetry incident I had remembered recently, which helped me understand why I stopped writing at an early age.

When I was fourteen years old and in the eighth grade at Hermosa Junior High in Farmington, New Mexico, Mrs. Ogden, our English teacher, had organized us to publish a literary magazine. We had been writing a lot since seventh grade, but here was our chance to put our work together and announce ourselves to the world as writers. We spent most of the year compiling our creative efforts, and were terribly proud of what we were doing. As a matter of fact, when I went back to a reunion of that high school in the summer of 2008, I was surprised to learn that four of us still had our copies of that magazine, and my classmates had the same warm feeling that I did about the experience.

When the magazine was finally published, five of my poems and a short story were included, and I was thrilled. I ran home with the magazine to show my dad, and bubbled out, "Daddy, Daddy, guess what? I'm a writer. Teacher says so. We did this literary magazine and I published a short story, and five poems."

He just looked at me for a long moment, then slammed his fist angrily on the arm of his chair and shouted, "Poems! You little shit, you'll never amount to anything."

Part of me died in that moment, and I felt myself shrivel up inside. I was shocked at his cruel words. I was horrified by the anger in his voice, and the terminal pronouncement. I stopped writing, except for required papers in school, and was sad at the loss. I thought that was the source of my writer's block. It was hugely damaging, but wasn't the only reason I stopped writing. I didn't know that until later.

Now in late 1986 I was frustrated, and wrote a poem, entitled "And Then I Stop."

The desire to express,
I was taught to repress,
Has caused me a block,
I wish to unlock.

> I pick up the pen,
> Start writing again,
> I feel the flow,
> And then I stop.

I was willing to take extra steps to explore why my creativity kept shutting down. At an ACA twelve-step retreat, I announced that I would be over in an empty room during an open space of time after the regular meetings. I wanted to talk about blocked creativity, and invited anyone who was interested to join me. About fifteen people showed up, which surprised me – I wasn't the only one with issues around my creativity. I shared my poem and talked about the poetry incident with my dad. Others shared similar incidents. It was heartening to know I wasn't alone, but didn't lessen the frustration.

That about summed up my attitude toward the writer's block at that time – frustration. Sometimes I have a long lag before I realize what I'm really feeling deep inside. There might have been more on the emotional side, but I couldn't access it right then. When the writing would dry up, I wasn't sure what to do about it. But I could feel down inside somewhere, that part of me was enormously relieved not to be publishing a book. That seemed odd, but at the time, I didn't know why I would feel that way.

Around this time, I ran across a book in the library that talked about Post-Traumatic Stress Disorder (PTSD). It was only recently recognized as a formal diagnosis, and this was the first I'd heard about it. The short definition was – exposure to a traumatic event in which the person experienced, witnessed or was confronted with an event that involved actual or threatened death or serious injury, and the person's response involved intense fear, helplessness or horror. That was a real mouthful of definition, but it was the symptoms list that really caught my attention.

The definition described a lot of stress responses that sounded really familiar. A person would have flashbacks, where they re-experienced the trauma. I'd had a couple of instances where I felt like I was living through some event I couldn't remember. A person would have feelings of estrangement or detachment from others – I had a strong sense that I was separate from other people. The definition discussed heightened arousal – which could lead to difficulty falling or staying asleep. I would lie down at 11 p.m. and suddenly be wide awake for several hours.

The list included anger issues – which I had been confronted about in my life. There was also a condition called hypervigilance – I was quick to feel like I was threatened or on high alert, even when no threat was around. An exaggerated startle response was very familiar to me – a balloon popping behind me could make me really jump and strike out in reflex. I struggled with feelings of guilt or shame, mistrust and feeling betrayed, stomach issues, substance abuse issues, and suicidal thoughts. I was experiencing all of those symptoms, but I didn't have a life-threatening event I could point to. Between the PTSD definition looking so familiar, and the writer's block, some odd things were happening in my world.

Things got even more bizarre. At the same time I contacted Claudia Black's publishing company, I had sent a query to Health Communications Inc. That publishing company had just brought out several books about ACA issues, including *Struggle For Intimacy*, by Dr. Janet Woititz. Once again, the books were by therapists, and not by someone who had grown up with alcoholism sharing their personal experiences, as I did with *Search For Peace*.

Health Communications requested a full manuscript, which I provided. They responded positively, commented favorably on the manuscript, and suggested some revisions. I agreed with their directions, and did a complete rewrite of the book at their request. Now I had a second publisher interested in my book. I had walked away from the first one. Would it happen again? This was another exciting prospect, a publisher who was interested in my personal account of the effects of growing up with an alcoholic.

I felt myself resist the possibility with Health Communications. After I submitted the rewrite, we agreed that it still needed some cleanup and editing. By that time, I once again told myself "I've lost the thread of the book." I stopped communicating with them, and for the second time – walked away from a publisher.

I had said I had writer's block, but now a new thought occurred to me. Was my block about writing, or about actually getting a book published?

Chapter 7: Testing My Writing Ability

It was September of 1988, and I had signed up for a creative writing class at the University of Houston. The teacher was a well-known published author and writing teacher from New York City who had agreed to guest lecture for a year. It was a great opportunity and I wanted to learn more about my craft, so on the first day I sat nervously in class with thirty other students. I was thirty-eight years old at the time, and felt a bit awkward because I was so much older than most of the students. I was willing to accept that discomfort to gain some insight about my writing ability.

In the first class the teacher described our writing process. We would each turn in a thousand-word piece of writing every two weeks. The teacher would select a few of our writings, and then the class and teacher would review and critique our work. That made my heart race. I had been journaling extensively, had written some short works and won praise for them, but this was unveiling my talent at a whole new level.

The teacher then opened a discussion by asking, "What is a story?" She suggested that we begin by defining the word. Several people responded. I took a minute to think about the meaning, and then raised my hand and said, "A story is something that happens to someone." The teacher smiled broadly, nodded, and said, "That's it exactly - at the very basic level, the essence of a story is action."

The class was an hour and a half long. The teacher would lecture for the first part of class, then read one of our works, and the class would spend ten to fifteen minutes reviewing it. We reviewed three to four pieces per class, and the group was very generous in their comments – honest but gentle. The teacher was a bit more direct – she got to the heart of the matter candidly and sometimes a bit harshly.

My first piece was not read aloud in class. It was a description of an empty house I discovered one time as I was exploring the countryside, which had open doors and possessions strewn all over the floor, signs of a rapid and turbulent departure. I planned to expand the story in future chapters. At the bottom, the teacher had written, "It's a great description, but is it a story?" I remembered the earlier discussion – I hadn't set in motion action and conflict that would make it a story.

I worked hard on a second piece entitled "The Hunt," about an experience I had as a fourteen-year-old deer hunting with my dad and his friends. The story was about how frightened I had been around grown men who were combining poker, whiskey, and guns in a very unsafe environment. I really put myself out there with the topic.

When the teacher said aloud "The Hunt," I felt my heart begin to race and my breathing grow rapid. I didn't know what to expect. As she read the class was very quiet. She finished, looked up and asked for comments. The class raved. "Insightful … brilliant … I could feel myself being there." I waited for the teacher's opinion. She went through the piece quoting passages and showing how wonderfully she felt the story unfolded and was portrayed. She said it was almost like the narrator was outside the experience, standing and looking on at the events. At the end the young boy has a living nightmare, where he visualizes the men running down the road after a deer, one of them tripping and falling and shooting his father in the back. The teacher was effusive in her praise of this part. One of her benchmarks about stories was: "Did it earn the ending?" With this piece, her answer was very strong. "Yes. This story absolutely does earn the ending."

I had tensely been listening and making notes all over my copy of the story. I looked at my watch and realized that forty-five minutes had elapsed. I left class that day with a new appreciation for my writing gift – it had been confirmed in a way that none of my friends could make me believe. A published author – a professional in the writing business – had raved about my work.

I thought maybe it was a fluke until it happened a second time, on a piece I had written entitled "Fight Night," about my dad introducing me to boxing. After some minimal lessons, my dad signed me up for Friday Night Fights at the YMCA, where I got beaten and humiliated by another young child. The teacher took about forty minutes to go through that short piece, and she praised it as effusively as the hunting story. She also showed great respect for me by asking me what I thought about the piece. With the other students, she just let the class critique and added her thoughts. But for me it was a much more mature dialogue.

"So what did you see about this piece? Is there anything you would want to improve?"

I gave my thoughts, and she agreed with the improvements I suggested. "Why don't you take on tightening this piece as your next project? I know you can make it even more powerful."

If the teacher had dismissed my work as not being that good, I might have been secretly relieved at being able to give up this need to write. What I discovered in creative writing class was the opposite. I had a gift, and it was my job to steward that gift – to share it in appropriate ways. That was a far scarier prospect than the possibility of having no talent.

That class affected me deeply. I could dismiss and block out when my friends said I had a writing talent. I could walk away and avoid it when publishers said I had a writing talent. But when a well-known published author raved about my work – it hit me in the gut. It was a dramatic confirmation of my writing ability. Moreover – if I didn't pursue writing I wasn't stewarding my God-given talent, and that just didn't sit right with me. I had to find out why my writing kept getting locked up.

Part Two

Nothing Left to Lose

Chapter 8: Ghosts Of The Wheat Harvest

"I'm going to quit my job and go work on the wheat harvest." Seriously, did I just say that? I was forty-one years old, and had arranged to go to Oklahoma, live in a trailer with a bunch of farm kids, and drive a grain truck. Was I crazy, or what?

As part of my healing journey I needed to explore my dad's story. I had never really known what happened to him during a critical time of his life, when he was reported to have gone off to work the wheat harvest. I blurted out my intention to go work on harvest while I was at dinner one night with several friends from church. One of them was a very solid individual, a leader at our church, and as an accountant, very grounded. Looking back, I realized later that I had secretly hoped because he was level headed, he would put down the idea, so I could give up on the whole thing. His answer blew me away.

"Dan, I think it's a great idea. It's part of your healing. I say go for it!"

So now I was getting support for the idea. How did I get myself into this?

In the fall of 1990, I was meeting with my friends Randy and Gregg on a regular basis to explore our dreams and aspirations. We had gotten to know each other while playing on the same softball team. Randy was bearded and stout, and a great pitcher. He was fascinated by the Lewis and Clark travels, and was reading all about them. Gregg was fast and nimble, and played next to me in the outfield. He was a math teacher who went hiking a lot, and had an ultimate goal to hike the Appalachian Trail.

Every two weeks, we gathered at a Chinese buffet and talked for several hours about things we'd like to do some day. It was at the time of the Men's Movement, where men went off for Hairy Man weekends and similar functions to "find themselves." I didn't buy into most of it, but Randy gave me a newsletter that had an article entitled "Finding Our Fathers." The premise was that boys grew into men with a wounded father within them, because they experienced their fathers as rejecting, incompetent, or absent figures. The article suggested that one way to heal the wounded father within was to plunge into the father's history. A man needed to find ways to empathize with his father's pain. I found that statement compelling, but little did I realize at the time the profound influence it would have on the direction of my life.

In December I began to write a story about the time my dad had disappeared. When I was seventeen, we moved briefly to

Oklahoma City, and my dad's world hit a low point – his drinking had spiraled out of control. My aunt and uncle came and got my mom, my sisters, and me, and moved us back to Fort Worth. We had to leave my dad behind, because he was unwilling to do anything about his problem. He disappeared for almost a year. I realized many years later I never expected to see him again – I wondered if we had lost him forever, and the thought pained me deeply.

My dad had lost his job, lost his family, lost everything. All we ever heard about that time of his life was that he had reportedly gone to work on the wheat harvest, which he had done one summer when he was in high school. Months later he returned to Fort Worth, fumbled around for a while, sobered up and got into recovery. Within ten years he had earned back the position he had once held in the oil industry, reunited the family, and had a totally different life than I would have expected when he disappeared. Something happened while he was on wheat harvest that changed his life – but I had no idea what. He had died before I could ask him.

I began to write the story of what might have happened to him, and after the first two chapters, realized that there was a very powerful story unfolding. I wrote the book as a fictional account, because casting it as a novel would give me needed distance from the story. But there was a missing piece – I had no idea what he went through working on the wheat harvest, which would have been especially tough for a middle-aged man. One night as we sat at the Chinese restaurant, with dinner dishes clanking in the background, and people walking by headed for the buffet, I said, "You know, some day, if I'm ever going to finish this book, I have to go work on the wheat harvest."

Randy nodded, a reflective look on his face. Then he said, "Dan, I've waited for a while to say anything. I don't know if you realize it, but that's the third or maybe fourth time you've mentioned going on wheat harvest." I was very surprised. I hadn't realized that I talked about it that much, and wasn't sure where he was headed with this. Randy was very thoughtful, and considered things carefully before he spoke. He continued. "I just want to let you know that, some day, if you ever want to go experience the wheat harvest to finish your book, I have relatives in Oklahoma who work the wheat harvest every year. I could probably get you on with them."

I can still remember hearing those words, and how I did a huge mental gulp at the time. I reacted like I usually do when I'm in shock – I sat there with a blank look on my face, saying nothing. I had been talking about a theoretical idea far in the future, and it had just been put into the realm of the possible – something that could actually happen. I reflected about this opportunity for a long time, because the spiritual ante had been greatly upped on the whole book project.

A couple of days later, I made a phone call. "Hey Randy, it's me. How's it going?"

"Pretty good, partner, how are things for you?"

"Good here. I think I have to go for it, though. I believe I'll take you up on that offer to contact your relatives – I think I have to go on the wheat harvest."

"Good for you, Dan. I thought I might be hearing from you. Let me get in touch with my cousins in Oklahoma, and I'll let you know."

———

The momentum built, and in May of 1991 I quit my job, drove to Oklahoma, and began living in a trailer with six high school farm kids, as I learned how to drive a huge grain truck. I could tell that this was a huge turning point in my life – which proved to be an understatement. I found my story, but more importantly, I walked in my dad's shoes – I understood the despair of working your way north on a harvest crew, believing you would never return home. Lying in my bunk when it was too rainy to work, resting up while the kids were out playing, I felt the weight of that certainty on a very visceral level. Because of the wreckage he had caused to the family, the embarrassment to friends and people he worked with, my dad would have believed going north was a one-way road. It was heartbreaking to contemplate – I tried to imagine what it must have been like for him, alone and closed off from all he had ever known.

It was a magical summer in many ways, but tough. I had worked in the oilfields for a couple of summers, but harvest was much harder. When the wheat was ripe and rain was forecast, we would work until 3 a.m., then get up at 7 a.m. and do it all over again. I was a forty-one-year-old man, trying to keep up with high school kids, which was very draining. My dad would have been forty when he went on harvest, and the impact of that sank in, as I grew more and more exhausted, physically and mentally.

By August 1991, I had gotten through the learning part, which had been pretty stressful, and knew what was going on with the work process. We had followed the wheat north as it ripened, and I was driving on a dirt road outside of Rapid City, South Dakota, taking the back roads to Sturgis, our next stopping point. I was at the wheel of a longbed grain truck pulling a combine on a trailer, a powerful experience that would have been unthinkable several months before. The long flowing vistas of hills and prairie grass that we drove by were enchanting, and the land started to look eerily familiar.

We pulled up to a T intersection, and the rig ahead of me had turned left, to the west. At the intersection, I was struck by a thought: "This looks like the scenes from *Dances With Wolves*." There was a long flat vista of grass to the north, which gently sloped down to a distant tree-lined valley. It was a beautiful, expansive vista.

The next day in Sturgis, I found out why the scene had looked so familiar – I had been looking down at the valley where the Indian village scenes were filmed in *Dances With Wolves*. Later, I got to tour the movie location. It was just that kind of summer, of magical and unusual events.

I stayed over with the crew and worked the fall harvest in Kansas, to continue to absorb the experience – I hadn't seen everything necessary to understand what Dad went through. According to the family legends, the "something" which happened to my dad had been in Kansas. I felt closer to his story there, and stayed longer.

I came home from harvest changed, but didn't know why or in what way. It was like standing really close to an impressionist painting – I was too close to the harvest experience to see the big picture. All I could see at that point were the individual brush strokes. It took several months over the winter to begin to see the whole experience clearly enough to start writing the book. I wrote the first half of the manuscript over the winter, but couldn't see the ending, and was still missing a few pieces.

I went on harvest a second year, in the summer of 1992, and got the final piece. I found a country church, that represented where a desperate man might have gone for solace, and the rest of the story began to formulate and come into focus. It became clear what might have happened which could convince my dad to return home and face the wreckage that he had created – he missed his family, and knew he needed to make things right.

I had a title, *Nothing Left To Lose*, and I now knew what the story would be. I was about to finish my next book. Then it would be time to get it published – the point which had tripped me up before.

Chapter 9: The Query Letter and The Question

B y 1994 the manuscript of *Nothing Left To Lose* was finished. It had unfolded as a very powerful story that I really wanted to share with the world. The manuscript had gone through several rewrites and extensive editing. It was time to explore publication, and I wanted to get perspective on the current state of the publishing industry.

I found a Leisure Learning Class in Houston about bringing a book to publication, taught by a marketing specialist named Joe Vitale. I signed up for it. It was a very informative course – Joe had a lot of great ideas and insights about publishing, and he was quite candid and direct with his opinions about how to approach getting a book published. Joe was very enthusiastic in his presentations, and I learned about an interesting shift in the industry.

The publishing industry had undergone a significant transition in recent years. Publishers were almost exclusively using literary agents to evaluate manuscripts, and would no longer review work directly submitted by authors. An author had to get an agent to represent their manuscript, and then the agent would pitch it to the publishers.

The query letter was more important than ever. It was still a brief sales presentation – the author had one page to convince an agent to request a copy of the manuscript. There were a lot of manuscripts being submitted, so the query letter had to be very effective to avoid the slush pile (where letters got tossed and lost), which was now in the agent's office, rather than at the publisher. There was a very short window of time to appeal to the initial reader, to keep their interest long enough to request a copy of your manuscript. Joe had confirmed this in the course.

I had what felt like a solid idea. After class one day, I went up to Joe and asked if he was available for consultations. I told him I had a manuscript I wanted to publish, and that I would like some help drafting a query letter for the agents. He was willing to help, and I gladly paid for an hour of his time to meet with me and draft a letter.

We sat down over coffee at a Denny's on the North Loop in Houston. I briefly described my book, and Joe went to work. First, he focused on finding the true essence of the story. In my initial query letter, I had made the wheat harvest the central theme. Joe politely suggested we put that into a secondary role – the true heart of the book was the man on harvest, and the shift he undergoes which allows him to return home. He helped me draft and refine my opening paragraph, because, in his opinion, we had to grab the reader quickly, or we'd be risking the slush pile.

The initial paragraph became:

Nothing Left To Lose, *a 68,000-word novel set in 1967, tells the riveting, complex story of Pat Waters, a dynamic salesman whose life has been nearly destroyed by his drinking. He hides from his past within the gritty world of a wheat harvesting crew, but has a powerful spiritual experience that reverses the course of his life.*

I was getting pretty excited by this point. We developed a very professional presentation, and I was quite pleased.

Then came the awkward moment. Joe asked, "So is the first time you've tried to have a book published?"

"No, I wrote a book back in 1985 that I sent off to publishers."

"Not this book?"

"No, another one. It was more of my personal story, and it was called *Search For Peace.*"

"So what happened with that book?"

"I had a couple of publishers interested, and even did a rewrite of the book for one of them."

"Publishers were interested in the book? How interested?"

"Well, one publisher called and started describing how he wanted to market the book, how he would price it. He read several passages from my manuscript back to me, and said they were very, very good. He was really excited, and wanted to move forward."

"And the other publisher?"

"They wanted me to do a rewrite from a more recovery-oriented perspective."

By this time Joe had a very odd, puzzled look on his face, as he asked, "So what happened? Did one of them publish it for you?"

I could feel myself getting embarrassed and said, "No, I sort of lost the thread of the book, and didn't follow up with them."

Joe's eyes got a little wider. "So you had two publishers interested in your book, wanting to publish it, and you never followed through?" Then came the inevitable and obvious question. "Why not?"

I shrugged. "I'm not sure. I just felt like I had lost touch with the story, and sort of ran out of momentum." My answer felt lame even to me. I was getting embarrassed.

"Did you ever follow up later, after you'd had a chance to rest up and get a fresh perspective?"

"No, I didn't."

Then he got to the heart of it. He stared off into space for a moment, then looked back at me and asked, "So how are you going to make sure the same thing doesn't happen again with this book?"

It was the question that I would have asked anyone else, and I knew it was a vital question to answer. But I didn't have anything substantial to say. I mumbled that I'd been working through the issues that led me to walk away from that book. "I don't think it will happen that same way again."

Joe looked at me skeptically, just as I was listening to my answer skeptically.

He sat quietly for a long time looking out the window, then said, "I think there is something underneath that previous experience with a publisher that absolutely needs to be addressed. Right now is not the time to try and deal with it, but it's pretty obvious it could happen again. You've got to sort this out, Dan."

I felt so awkward that I just said, "Yes, I agree with you Joe."

I thanked him for his time, and we went our separate ways. But the meeting had ended on a down note, and I could feel it. A tremendously significant question had been exposed to the light, where I couldn't hide it, couldn't avoid dealing with it. How was I going to make sure I didn't walk away from publication again? I had no clear answer.

Chapter 10: Facing Publication Again

I t was time to publish the novel *Nothing Left To Lose*. I sent query letters to a list of literary agents likely to be interested in the book. I was so scared when I put the queries in the mail that my arms were shaking. A friend had to go with me for support, just to be there when I actually mailed the letters.

I knew I would be getting responses from the publishers soon. Why was I so scared to find out if they liked my manuscript? There it was again – I could feel a deep, black fear when I moved forward with the publication process.

For several weeks, I waited anxiously for replies, and was delighted when five literary agents asked for the manuscript. Things were looking very positive. The fear didn't feel as overwhelming, and I hoped maybe – just maybe – we'd broken the chains of the old childhood fears.

I happily sent off copies of my manuscript, as other replies came in – mostly rejections. Since I already had several positive responses, the rejections sure didn't sting quite as bad. One of the agents suggested the book needed professional editing, and recommended an editing service. The agent said she would like to see my manuscript after it had been edited and revised. It got interesting when a second agent said the book needed editing and suggested the same editing company. All the literary agents who requested the manuscript recommended editing and polishing.

I took it as a sign when the two literary agents suggested the same editing service, so I did some research, and the company looked solid. I called the editor, and made arrangements to have him edit *Nothing Left To Lose*. Things were really moving forward – there were agents waiting, and I was connected to a professional editor. I promptly sent my manuscript to the editor. I sent follow-up letters to the literary agents who had shown interest, to let them know I was in process of revising the manuscript, and would resubmit as soon as it was finished. I assured the two agents who had suggested the same editor that I was using his services, and told them they would be pleased with the outcome.

Two months later the editor returned my manuscript marked up where changes were needed, along with a two-page evaluation. The editor had been a couple of weeks late in completing the work. He said their office had been ransacked and they had lost a lot of files and notes. Since he was late, he made me an offer. When I revised my manuscript, he would evaluate it a second time – at no cost to me – to double-check the changes and ensure that we had crafted a solid novel. I was thrilled with that offer.

The fear was pushing on me, but not so fiercely, because I hadn't gotten that close to publication. First I had to go through the revision process, and then have the agent accept my manuscript, before we began offering it to publishers.

I was in agreement with the changes suggested by the editor, so I went to work on a major revision of the manuscript. Sometimes I felt stuck, like I physically could not sit down to work on revisions. At times it was completely frustrating. I got up from my desk after one more dry session where I couldn't put words on paper, and angrily declared: "If I can't break through this writing block shit, I'm just going to give up writing and take up golf."

It took several months to make changes, and then I sent the fully revised manuscript back to the editor. The novel felt complete. I was highly confident that the editor would sign off on my revisions, and suggest that it was ready to be resubmitted to the agents. I was pretty tense, and waited with great anticipation.

One day I got the revised manuscript in the mail. I opened it, glanced at the two-page evaluation, and then began flipping through the manuscript. I was appalled at all the red marks and notes I saw. I sat down, stunned. Finally I picked up the evaluation, and it felt like I had lost ground with the novel – the changes suggested and the direction of the novel felt completely different.

The crushing blow was the song. The title of the book was based upon the Janis Joplin song, "Me And Bobby McGee," and the lyric line "Freedom's just another word for *Nothing Left To Lose.*" The song had played on the radio at a critical point in the novel, and had affected the main character deeply. The novel was set in 1967, and the person editing the manuscript had observed that this particular song didn't come out until 1971. Since the novel was a fictional account of events that had happened to my dad in 1967, it felt wrong to move it forward in time just to fit the song. Why hadn't this been brought up during the first evaluation?

I was reeling from the huge amount of work now facing me to revise the novel – again. Then I started to look more closely at the red marks and notes. The handwriting didn't look quite right. It quietly registered that the same person didn't do this evaluation. But that got lost in the enormous disappointment that my novel – which I had thought was complete – needed yet another complete rewrite[1]. The whole thing was so demoralizing it would be a long time – eight years – before I could bring myself to write again creatively.

As I looked at the revisions returned by the editor I felt defeated, and didn't have the energy to fight both the revision process and the writer's block, to finish this novel. I did the only thing that made sense at the time – I went and bought some golf clubs.

[1] I discovered many years later that this editing service was part of a shady arrangement – several agents were purported to be receiving kickbacks from the editor for suggesting his services to writers. His company had been sued for non-performance several times. Apparently low-paid apprentices, in a high-volume, low-quality operation, many times did the editing. At a writer's conference I met a credible book editor from New York. When I told him this story, he laughed and said it was a big industry scandal for a while. He said I was lucky to actually have received an evaluation.

Part Three

Mamaw Enters The Picture

Chapter 11: What Mamaw Told Me

W hen I gave up my dream of being a writer I was devastated. I tried to look in other directions and stay busy, and not feel how much it hurt. I felt a tremendous ache in my heart to feel my dream die. It was worse because I was so completely powerless to do anything about it. I felt disoriented a lot of the time, I was sad when I allowed myself to feel it, and felt generally frustrated.

"I think I'll just go to the driving range today and hit a few balls." It was all I could think to do, when I didn't have a writing project to work on.

Something was locking up my writing, but I had no idea what. I spent several pretty miserable years not writing creatively, and journaling very little. It was painful to try and write, fearing I would never solve the mysterious hangup that had killed my destiny. I could feel how the pain and frustration festered, like acid churning down in my gut.

I moved to Albuquerque, New Mexico, in 2002, a return to the part of the country where I grew up. I started working with a healer – not exactly a therapist, but someone who worked more intuitively. She came highly recommended, and with nothing to lose, I decided to give her methods a try.

When she asked what I wanted to work on, I immediately said creativity. After some preliminary discussion while she took notes, she performed some work on me. She let herself empathically connect with me and sense my energy in a way I didn't fully understand. She concluded there was something deeply buried in my subconscious, which had to do with writing. I had always thought my writer's block was because of my dad shaming my poetry when I was fourteen. My dad had wanted to be a writer, but had kept it secret from the family for many years. Was his writing shamed as well? I had never considered another cause for my difficulties around writing, but evidently something else had happened. I was desperate at this point, so I decided to try another exercise to access the scared little boy inside me.

In 1988, just after my dad died, I had remembered a particularly violent incident with my dad when I was a teenager. The violence happened in 1967, and twenty-one years later I had brought it to the surface by accessing the memories of my inner child. I did what had been described as a Gestalt, or empty chair, exercise. I had a man from my therapy group come to my apartment for support. He just sat and watched. I set two chairs a few feet apart, and sat down in one chair. I spoke from that chair as the adult, and talked to my inner child, asking him to tell me what had happened. Then I would stand up and go and sit in the other chair.

From that chair I answered as the child. It was eerie how my voice changed – it got higher and quavered. I could feel the tremendous fear of the child as the events were described.

This is what the inner child revealed during that Gestalt exercise:

In 1967, we were living in Oklahoma City, having moved there in a desperate attempt by my parents to clean up their drinking problems. My dad's drinking had progressed to the point where he was at risk of losing his job. I had taken a job as a busboy at a local hamburger restaurant. I came home late one frigid winter night, and found my dad alone in the living room with a loaded rifle. I later realized he had been about to commit suicide when I walked into the room. He got an ugly look on his face, and asked me, "Where have you been?"

I was shocked at the way he asked the question, and that he didn't remember about my new job – my first job. I told him I had been at work. He sat for a moment, then with a low, hard-edged voice which chilled me more than if he had yelled, said, "Don't you ever think you're better than me, just because you have a job." He then beat me, and picked up his hunting rifle, pointing it at me as he told me to get out of his sight. I walked out of the room expecting a bullet in my back. I spent the night in my room waiting for him to come in and shoot me, and only fell into a restless sleep at dawn. At that point the memory and inner child exercise ended.

The violence was directly about me being successful. The message was that if I were to succeed, my dad would kill me. It explained a lot of bizarre things in my world – I had sabotaged my career a number of times, and tried hard not to succeed.

What was revealed during that inner child exercise had been a key in helping heal my world. It was so successful, it was time to try something similar about the writing issue – I had nothing to lose, since I wasn't able to write anyway.

With the deep block I was currently facing, I was willing to do whatever I could, so in October 2003 I drove up to Farmington, the small town in Northwest New Mexico where I had lived from ages five through sixteen. I had some very good memories about that town – it was the place where my inner child last remembered the feeling of being safe. The safest place of all – in that town or any town – was the library. Librarians were the ultimate arbiters of quiet and safety. Even as a young child I knew that if something bad were to happen at the library, the librarian would handle it – calling the police if necessary. After checking into a motel, I drove over to the library and walked inside.

Since I was going to be in a public place, it felt right to do the inner child work as a written exercise. I was comfortable with the process, and felt I could make the exercise work without using the chairs. The need for safety seemed more important than the method at this point – it signaled how deep and painful this memory would be.

I walked to the back of the library, looked around and found an empty table away from others, where I could be quiet and not be disturbed. I placed my legal pad and pen on the table and sat down. I took a deep breath, quieted my mind, and allowed myself to relax. After a few minutes I felt ready to start, so I picked up the pen and began to write to my inner child, who I had named Little Danny Fear Child. As I wrote from the adult perspective, I sensed that the child answering was eight years old, and I could visualize a frightened young child curled up in a corner. I was hoping to set him free, so we could let go of the Fear Child part.

"Danny. Are you ready to tell me what I can't see, about why I get locked up with my writing? You know – the thing the therapist said was really buried. Danny, it's time for me to write. Therefore I must let go of that old block. Can you understand that? You are safe now. I will take care of you. Letting go of this block will lead to great, great joy. Are you all right with all of this? If you are, just tell me – just blurt it out – no shame, no blame."

Danny spoke. "I was afraid if I wrote something, and someone read it, they might not like me because I said what I saw. People would know what was going on in our family. They would know our family was not all fine, and someone would get mad at me."

"What else? Go deeper – what's underneath that?"

"You really want to know?"

"Yes, I do. Please tell me."

"I always loved to read. I wanted to write stuff like that. I knew I would be good at it."

"Yes?"

"If I wrote a book and people read it, they might think I was weird or something, and not want to be around me. And I'd be lonely. I wouldn't be like all the other people who didn't write – and I'd be alone – again. I've been alone too much and I didn't want that. So I would not write."

"Why would you be alone?"

"Because writers are crazy – everybody knows that. And nobody wants to be around them."

"Who told you that?"

"Mamaw did."

"When?"

"When I went to visit her in Fort Worth. She asked me what I wanted to do when I grew up. I told her I wanted to write books. She said I didn't want to do that. Writers were crazy and people wouldn't want to be around me. They might have to put me away – lock me up somewhere. I didn't want that."

"Where were you when she told you that?"

"We were in her house."

"How did it feel when she said that?"

"I felt smothered by her always, but right then I felt killed."

"What did she look like when she said it?"

"She saw the look on my face, and she smiled. It was a cruel, 'I won' kind of smile."

"What did that feel like, seeing her face?"

"My stomach hurt, and I wanted to cry."

"Is there anything else?"

"Well, she kept saying it – all that week – until I wanted to go to Big Mommy's to get away. But I couldn't tell anyone about it."

"Why not?"

"Because Mamaw was a nurse, and she had heard it from Doctor Crowder, that creepy old guy she worked for. She said only those kind of people knew about stuff like this. She said don't tell anyone. They might think you were crazy just for asking and lock you up for that."

"Danny."

"Yes?"

"Do you understand that what she said was not true?"

"Kind of. Sort of."

"Remember what Mom said about writers one time?"

"Sort of."

"She said that writers were held in the highest regard. That they were revered in the world she grew up in – they were tremendously respected. Remember that?"

"Yes, I remember. But Mamaw was so sure. I didn't know what to believe."

"I understand. But it was true, and it is true. You will not be called crazy and get locked up if you are a famous writer. You will be honored, revered, and respected as a person who sees and speaks truth. That is the truth. We'll take all the time you need for you to get comfortable with that. Alright?"

"Yeah, OK. I like that. Will you remind me?"

"Of course I will. How are you feeling?"

"My stomach doesn't hurt so much."

"Why do you think that is?"

"Because I really, really want to write, and it made me very sad when I knew I wasn't supposed to."

"So you could write all along, but you thought you should not?"

"Oh yes, I could write any time I wanted to. I had fun with the stuff we wrote in junior high. But there was, you know, the crazy thing. So it was safer not to write, because I didn't want to get locked up."

"Danny, you just relax, and enjoy thinking about writing. You and I will release that old belief. So you can write freely and fully – with joy."

"I can do that. I am happy now."

———

Mamaw. Who was this woman? She was Ruth Fox, the mother of my dad, a small woman with brown hair streaked with grey. She was from a poor family in a small country town, and was not well-educated or very worldly. She was an office manager for a doctor, but told everyone she was a nurse. She lived alone in a small, cramped house on Hazeline Street on the east side of Fort Worth. She was terribly needy after her husband Pat Hays left many years ago, following a vicious and ugly scene, which I heard about years later.

Pat had decided to leave her, and tried to walk out of the house. His two sons, Ben and George, dutifully went out and got into their dad's car in the driveway. Mamaw threw herself at his feet, and wrapped her arms around his leg. She screamed at him, begging him not to leave, sobbing hysterically. Neighbors came out on their porches and watched with horrified expressions, as the man dragged a woman on his leg out the front door of the house.

Pat hit her several times on top of the head, trying to break free, yelling at her to let him go. George jumped out of the car and tried to stop his dad from hitting his mom. Ben watched in horror from the car, frozen with shame. Finally Pat broke free of Mamaw, and left her lying on the front porch sobbing, put George back in the car, and drove away.

Mamaw was terribly clingy and controlling after that – later the boys moved back in with her and she doted on them to an unnatural degree – she wanted them near her at all times. Ben (my dad), never got past the guilt of sitting passive in the car, and let Mamaw control him all through his adult life. She was very childlike, and craved constant attention. Even when my dad did something nice for her, it was never enough to satisfy her. She could be extraordinarily cranky and demanding if she didn't get her way – she would throw things across the room in frustration. She got giddy with childish joy at other times. Only later did I realize she was probably taking pills of some kind. She could be nasty – she enjoyed being mean. I'll never forget the ugliness in her grin when she pinched my arm really hard one evening. She laughed it off like she was being cute, but it wasn't – it really hurt. I never liked going to visit her. After doing the inner child exercise, I understood why I never felt safe around her.

Now I knew what – or rather who – had locked up my writing. I knew why I had walked away from publication. The writing exercise had just flowed easily, and hadn't taken that long. Little Danny had been ready to unburden the secret he had kept for over forty-five years. This revelation was a huge thing to absorb. What to do about it – I'd have to figure that out later. Right then I just wanted to let the truth sink in.

Chapter 12: I Capture The Writing Vision

After I got back the memory about Mamaw, that whole experience slipped below the surface for a while. It took some time to make it all real, to absorb the magnitude of the abuse, and the damage it had caused. I also suspect that I hoped the creative block had somehow broken loose and would just go away all by itself.

One time on the phone I told my friend Karen about the inner child exercise. I had known her for over twenty years, and she was one of the wisest and most intuitive people I had ever met. Though she had brown hair, Karen was from a family of redheads, and had inherited that spicy personality, so she wouldn't hesitate to dig in her heels for something she believed in. She was well-read and highly intelligent, and she was tuned in to what was going on with me to a degree I had never experienced before.

After I told her about the inner child work, she asked, "Where do you go from here? What are you going to do about the Mamaw message?" I didn't say much – I didn't really have an answer. When I had experiences that indicated I was still "locked up," Karen would remind me about the writer's block, and what had happened with

Mamaw. She felt that was a pivotal event, and needed to be addressed. For two years, I smiled and nodded when she brought it up, but wasn't willing to deal with it. When I wrote my next book, and got closer to publishing it, the incident with Mamaw shot up in my face where it could not be ignored.

That whole process for the next book I was to write started with a burst of inspiration. It was the fall of 2005. I had spent eight painful years not writing, and felt like the life had been sucked out of my soul. I decided to write again. I didn't know what to write about, how to get past the writer's block, or if I would walk away from another book. But it was time to give writing a try once more. The next topic unfolded through an extraordinary and powerful experience.

I had driven from Albuquerque to Texas to celebrate Thanksgiving with the family. Everyone had to get back to where they lived, so the holiday just naturally wound down early. Saturday morning I drove back to New Mexico, and I could feel something brewing during the long trip home. I had random thoughts flitting around my mind, but couldn't pull them together. I pulled in to my garage after the eleven-hour drive, got my suitcase out of the trunk, and went inside my condo, glad that the long journey was over. I had an extra day to rest before going back to work, and I would use the time to wind down, and see if I could collect my thoughts about the ideas that were formulating.

I took out a legal pad and started jotting some notes. In 1994, I finished a novel called *Nothing Left To Lose*, a fictionalized depiction of a time when my dad disappeared after his drinking spiraled out of control – and what I thought might have happened to him. He reportedly went to work on the wheat harvest, and came back very different – he had some kind of spiritual experience, and his whole world changed after that.

Something had always nagged me about the wheat harvest novel, and what had bothered me started to become clear. My dad passed away in 1987, and a lot happened over the next several years. I had remembered a series of violent incidents by my dad when I was a teenager, culminating with the gun incident late at night. I did a lot of recovery work about those issues. When I began writing the novel, it was from a very loving and respectful point of view regarding my dad. That was the problem – the wheat harvest novel was written at the end of a long, painful, and sometimes very angry road of recovery from those violent incidents. To just publish the harvest novel wouldn't tell the whole story.

There was an extensive backstory that needed to be told, and it would have to start before my dad's death. There was too much to tell in one book, because I would have to condense and compress too many topics to adequately address what I had gone through. If I were to write about working through my anger, that one topic would lead to a complex story. The time from 1987 when my dad died, to 1991 when I went on wheat harvest to find out about his story, was an incredibly dense period of my life.

I jotted down a tentative title for the first book: *Freedom's Just Another Word*. It would begin with the events leading up to my dad's death, and the time period after he died, where I remembered the most traumatic violent incident with him. That event had skewed and influenced my whole world for many years. I once told a friend I had a fear of failure. She looked at me oddly, and said, "It looks to me like you have a fear of success." That statement described my world before I remembered the violence. The message from the incident was – *If you succeed, I will kill you* – I worked hard to avoid looking successful.

When I was reading my journal notes in preparing to write this book, I discovered something I had written in 1988: *Someday I will have to write about the time around my dad's death, and the book needs to be entitled* Freedom's Just Another Word. I was shocked, because I had forgotten writing those words. My subconscious mind remembered the title, and brought it back to the light when it was needed.

The story really started with *Freedom's Just Another Word*, which would function as a bookend to the wheat harvest novel called *Nothing Left To Lose*. It felt symmetric that the two titles were from the same line in the Janis Joplin song "Me And Bobby McGee."

I began to sketch out the events that came between the first and last book, and suddenly realized that there were five more books to write. Tentative titles began to assign themselves to each book, almost as if I had known them all along, but wasn't aware of them on a conscious level.

The next book would be about what happened immediately after the events with my dad – how I began to reclaim my life. I didn't have a clear picture of that book, and I later realized there wasn't enough for a book during that time frame. My friend Karen suggested that a book about the events with my crazy grandmother Mamaw might need to be written next. *Healing The Writer – A Memoir About Overcoming PTSD* would describe my healing journey from the damage caused by Mamaw. It would explain many elements to be revealed in the later books, like always being worried that someone thought I was crazy.

The Tiger Unveiled. I had to address my anger, and how I resolved it. I had to talk about working through my feelings about the violent incident with my dad. Just after I remembered the violence, I had a dream about a tiger, which prompted the title of the book. I was in a new house I had bought, and discovered there was a tiger inside it. I told myself he was tame, but he came up and put his teeth on my arm, and I realized the tiger was not tame, and he would eventually destroy me. The tiger – I took that to be my anger and rage. I was sitting on a dangerous and explosive anger, which desperately begged to be addressed.

I was forced to deal with that anger because of a horrible incident that happened to me with some people from the recovery program I was in, not long after my dad died. A group of people came to my apartment late at night, and took me to Denny's. Their stated reason was to confront me about my pattern of backing away from people. Their motives were more complicated, and the hidden agenda was that someone had spread a rumor that I was at home about to commit suicide. The participants took the opportunity to dump a lot of anger on me. The ringleader many years later told me that no one deserved what happened to me that night.

After that event, I found out all the details of how that group formed and stirred themselves up enough to come after me, and it was pretty dysfunctional. I had a tangible target for my anger. The deeper well of my anger was the ticking time bomb of my issues with my dad. I didn't want to hurt anyone while I released those deep toxins, and those people were easy targets. I put myself under an Anger Contract, so I could safely release my anger. I did a lot of creative anger work – like spending a year in a boxing gym, tearing up a lot of paper to release my anger, driving down the road listening to Van Halen and screaming. It was a long and healing journey, but led to a miraculous new sense of peace for me.

Healing The Wounds. After the anger subsided, there was a period of healing, of coming to a peace and resolution about what happened with my dad. I engaged in a number of exercises to make peace – an imagined healing conversation with my dad, trips to Tulsa where he spent the last years of his life, and a long time of grieving how much we had both lost through his drinking and the horrible damage it caused.

The Symbolmakers. This book would be about the group of men I had gathered with. We spent a lot of time talking at a Chinese buffet, and those conversations fueled my desire and ability to go on the wheat harvest, and find out about my dad. Talking with those men was an incredible healing experience, and would help explain my ability to take the vision quest trip to work the wheat harvest.

Then I Went To Find My Father would be my own experience on the wheat harvest. It would reveal how I gradually came to an understanding about my dad's story and his experience. I walked in his shoes, metaphorically. It would be a different viewpoint of the wheat harvest experience – it would not be my dad's experience on harvest, but my own. As one friend said, "You think you're going on harvest to find out about your dad, but I think you're going to find out about Dan."

Nothing Left To Lose. With the previous books fleshing out the backstory – the wheat harvest novel would make a lot more sense.

By showing the backstory, and the healing journey, a wheat harvest novel about my dad written from a loving perspective would make more sense.

I was very clear that the damaging messages of Mamaw would need to be addressed – and if possible, somehow healed – if I was ever going to write those books. What I didn't know in that moment – writing the very first book in the series, *Freedom's Just Another Word*, would drive the issues caused by my grandmother up to the surface and into my face, where they could no longer be ignored. I would be forced to deal with Mamaw.

Chapter 13: The Creative River Flows Once More

W ith a burst of inspiration, I had sketched out a plan for a series of books I wanted to write. The creativity was flowing, so I began to flesh out the direction of the first book. The next weekend, I drove back up to Farmington, back to my safe place. I went to the library, took out my legal pad and pen, and settled down to capture the thoughts that had started to emerge.

I had a working title for the first book, *Freedom's Just Another Word*, and now began to put flesh on the bones of the idea. The book would revolve around the events at the time of my dad's death just before Thanksgiving in 1987. I was journaling extensively in those days, so I had a lot of notes to work from. The book would cover about four months, and include how I remembered the violent incident with my Dad, and began the process of healing that wound.

It became clear the book needed to start before my dad died, but I wasn't sure how far back in time to go. For a reason I couldn't pin down at that moment, the beginning point would be my visit to see a man named Wayne. He was a very charismatic Bible Study teacher who a group of us in Houston had followed for years. At one time he had taken me under his wing as someone he wanted to mentor.

In the fall of 1987 my life was falling apart. I was anxious and panicky a lot of the time, for no reason I could identify. I was broke, out of work, couldn't bring myself to go get a job, and was totally mystified as to why all of that was happening. I went to see Wayne for help and support. He planted seeds of doubt on my path of being a writer (which he had previously supported), said some harsh and critical things about me, and made some rather snide comments which slandered my integrity. In a normal world you'd say it was a bad call to go talk with him, don't do that again. My reaction was the key – I was really angry right after I left his office, but within three days was suicidal. That was why the book had to start with the visit to Wayne – that extreme overreaction signaled something very, very deep and dark going on in my life.

I fleshed out the main events of the book, and then began to write the opening scene. I decided to use first person. From the very first lines, the voice felt right – my words were measured and calm, and sounded very centered. I was not writing as the panicky young man who had gone into Wayne's office. I was writing from the perspective of someone who had done a lot of work to come to peace with the events I described, and just recounted what happened. That voice stayed very consistent as I wrote, and was easy to maintain. I wrote part of the opening scene as I sat at the library, which was easy because those events were still very vivid in my mind.

After fleshing out the events I wanted to include in *Freedom's Just Another Word*, then writing the first scene, I felt creatively tired. I had accomplished a lot in that trip, so I explored the town for the rest of the day, then drove back to Albuquerque the next morning. The writing continued over the next several months.

Each chapter of the book started with a process I called "loading the computer," the computer being my brain. I would read my journal entries for the time period I was going to write about, then let it simmer and percolate for a week or so, as I went about my daily life. One day I would feel ready, sit down at my desk, and out would flow a complete chapter, with scenes and dialogues, flashbacks and reflections, in a very coherent order. That happened all through the spring of 2006. I was a little surprised at how the writing continued to flow, given my experiences with the writer's block, but the process felt very natural and relaxed.

The hardest time to write about was the week my dad died. Almost nineteen years after his death, I had never sat down to write about everything that had happened. I had written about my dad's death, and how I felt about it, as part of my grief process. But I had never tried to put together my experience from the moment I got the phone call from my sister, "Come home, Dad is dying." It was tough to write, but flowed just like the rest of the book, and felt very cathartic.

While this was going on, I sold my condo and moved from Albuquerque back to Texas. I was having conversations with a man who ran a company in Houston where I had previously worked. He was going to create a job for me, supervising the startup of one element of a software module. In the summer of 2006, I had already put money down to hold an apartment in Houston, but the job didn't work out. I didn't want to move back to Houston if there was no job available, and at the very last minute I was in limbo and wondering what to do.

I moved back to Fort Worth, and was thrilled, because I had always wanted to return there some day. There had never been oil activity around the town, but much to my surprise there was a big oil and gas boom going on in North Texas. My skills as an oil and gas landman were in great demand. I began to work in the oil industry.

I really believe things would not have unfolded in the same way if the original job had worked out. Being in Houston would not have propelled the Mamaw issues to the surface with the same force and immediacy that happened in Fort Worth, where she had lived. Part of my connection to the city was my interactions with Mamaw, and living there allowed that abuse to surface more readily and completely. Driving by the house where she had lived made things immediate in a way that wouldn't have happened in Houston.

With the writer's block, my writing had been a fragile thing to hold on to at times, so I was surprised when I kept making progress on the book, even while relocating and starting a new job. Around the first of 2007, I had a handwritten draft of the first two-thirds of the book. I wanted to let the manuscript get really cold before I went back to look at it. I had a flash of inspiration, and asked my friend Karen if she would type up my notes, and I would pay her for it. She had worked as a legal assistant and was a fast typist. More importantly, she had a Master's in English with a creative writing specialty, and had worked as an editor for a college book publisher. She had an editor's perspective and a great feel for writing, which would be vital for me.

Karen and I had already talked about her editing my book for me, and this seemed a way to get a head start on that process. I mailed off my handwritten notes (chicken scratch is more like it – I'm left-handed and have lousy penmanship), which she had assured me she could read.

In March of 2007, I finished the last of the manuscript, and put the rest of my notes in the mail to Karen. It was time to study the publishing industry – for a third time – to see about getting that book published. I was moving forward – again. Would I stop short like I had done before? Would I walk away from a third book? I wasn't sure. I sensed that I was in a different place on the writer's block than I had been before. I was committed to doing whatever it took to get past the blocks, and actually publish a book. *Freedom's Just Another Word* felt like a crossroad – what I did with the book would indicate where I was with the writer's block.

Karen called me about that time. "Dan, I don't want to freak you out, but I have some feedback if you're ready."

I felt my muscles tighten. "Why, is it not any good?"

"No, that's not it at all. Dan, this is a really powerful book. It's very possible that this book will be very successful. We don't have to get into it right now, but I thought you'd want to know that much."

"Okay. I think that's all I can hear right now. But thanks for telling me."

"You're welcome."

We got off the phone, and I just sat there in shock for a while. Karen and I had discussed books and literature extensively, and I knew she had an extraordinary clarity about writing. I had just heard a powerful affirmation of my writing ability, from a source I really trusted. It was sure getting hard to deny my creative talent. Things were brewing for me to get to the bottom of the writer's block.

Chapter 14: The Writer's Conference and The Fear

In April 2007 I began to study the publishing industry – for the third book I wanted to take to publication. I wasn't sure if I would walk away from a book again. But I had to try. Mamaw saying "They'll call you crazy and lock you up" was much more of the reason to avoid publishing books than I had realized, and it was time to push past the damage of her words.

My research indicated writer's conferences could be very helpful in learning about the publishing industry, and offered an amazing opportunity, where writers could set up a brief meeting with a New York literary agent to pitch their manuscript. I found a conference in Austin, only three hours away, scheduled for June. I signed up, studied the list of agents available for pitch sessions, and sent in my top three choices.

Shortly after I signed up for the writer's conference, I began to have trouble sleeping. I would lay awake until very late at night, my legs shaking violently for a long time. I had a terrible feeling of doom – it felt like something really bad was about to happen. I was very anxious, my breathing quickened, and I wanted to run or escape – but from what, I did not know. When I had uncovered the violence with my dad, I had experienced something similar. I knew I must have touched something really deep – I just couldn't see right then what had been triggered – or why.

By the week of the conference, I was shaking with fear every night, was wide awake at 3 a.m., on high alert, and feeling more than fear – I was terrified that something horrible was about to happen. I would lie on my bed and listen intently – sure that someone was coming to get me, and harm me in some way. I was concerned that I would be so sleep deprived that I might not be able to participate fully in the conference. I drove to Austin with a knot in the pit of my stomach, my heart racing and feeling tremendously tense. I drove to the hotel, checked in, and got my conference materials.

I had signed up for a pre-conference workshop on the topic of creative nonfiction, presented by the keynote speaker for the weekend. I didn't know what the term meant, and wanted to find out. I walked in to the workshop, sat down next to a woman, and we chatted nervously for a few minutes. She hadn't finished a book, and was going to use her pitch session with an agent to ask which of three directions she might go with her manuscript. I was surprised, because I had read that it was important in pitch meetings to have a completely edited and marketable manuscript ready, in case it was requested.

I experienced the same thing a number of times over the weekend – authors who hadn't finished a book, and were just in an exploratory phase. I felt better about having completed my manuscript. Then I met an author who handed out business cards with his book cover on them, and a website listed. That opened my eyes to the business side of the writing life; I needed to get that part set up. The workshop was excellent, but the phrase creative nonfiction turned out to be writing memoir with the fiction elements of scenes and dialogue – the way I wrote. It looked like a new term for an old writing style.

I had dinner, came back to my hotel room, and tried to settle down. I shook with fear until about 2 a.m., and decided to skip the opening session. I started my morning by attending one of the early workshops at 10 a.m. There may have been great information presented, but I was so nervous about meeting the agent that I didn't remember much, and finally left the session to walk off some nervous energy. I went up to the second floor where the pitch sessions were taking place. There was a lot of noise and bustle, as authors paced nervously, waited, mentally rehearsed, and were escorted in and out of several breakout rooms by conference staff.

My turn came and I walked into a small room with four cocktail tables spaced far apart, where agents and authors were seated and talking. There was incredible tension in the quiet buzz of conversations. I sat down with the literary agent, shook her hand, and began my pitch. I was so nervous I felt like I was blabbering. I described my memoir, gave her some background on it, and then listened for her input. She compared my book to a memoir about a homeless man – a book totally unlike mine – and it was obvious that she didn't really understand what my book was about. I realized later that I had misrepresented my memoir, emphasizing the darker side first and making it sound ponderous, instead of highlighting the hopeful message later in the story. (Was I sabotaging myself unconsciously? I believe so.)

When she passed on representing the manuscript, I thanked her and left. I couldn't concentrate on another session, so I just walked around for a while. At first, mostly I felt numb. Underneath the numbness, I was devastated at being rejected – my heart hurt that the agent didn't want my book. I wanted to cry, or at least feel the pain, but I wasn't safe in the strange hotel in the middle of a conference, so I just stuffed it down. I hadn't met anyone I could share my intense disappointment with, so I just walked around with a gnawing ache that churned in my gut like bad food.

Late Saturday afternoon, after the last workshops and agent meetings, the conference hosted a happy-hour mixer in the lounge downstairs. The room was densely packed with people and very noisy, so I went out onto the porch to get some breathing room. I visited with several people, and then talked with a man I sat next to at lunch that day. He was visiting with a blonde-haired woman, and then she and I began to chat. Her name was Beth, and she asked about the book I had written. I told her how *Freedom's Just Another Word* started with me going to a spiritual mentor who was supposed to help me, but was very harsh toward me. Beth asked, "So was he trying to hold you accountable?"

"Yes, in one way you could say that, but the way he was talking was more like a putdown – like he was mad at me or something."

She nodded. "I see. And that was pretty hurtful to you?"

"It was, but the part where it got tied to the past was what happened after that. The guy said some rough things to me; sure it would make sense that I reacted to what he said and the way he phrased things. I was mad at the time – I wrote down everything he said, and was furious about it. But two days later, I was suicidal. That part didn't make sense – it was a more extreme response than the events warranted."

Beth nodded, listening intently. I could tell she understood what I was trying to say. "So what did you get out of all of that?" she asked, as people and conversations swirled around us on the now crowded patio.

"It wasn't apparent at the time what I got out of that exchange. The next thing that happened was that my dad died, and I had to deal with that." She nodded again, a sympathetic look on her face. "But through a whole sequence of events, I remembered a violent incident with my dad that took place when I was a teenager, which made the current things happening in my life make sense and fall into place."

"Wow," she said, shaking her head. "This sounds like a powerful book. You talk about it with such strength and conviction. You know, Dan, I just know God wants you to publish this book. I just get that. It is going to happen, and you're going to find a way to make it happen. You have to share this story."

I was stunned at the power of what she had just said. Her words were like a mandate or a call to action, and continued to resonate through my soul. The power of the story I had chronicled gave me fuel to keep moving forward, even through the fear, and the disappointment and pain that my initial contact with a literary agent had been so unsuccessful.

Chapter 15: What Is It About That Particular Park?

Going to the writer's conference had stirred up something very disturbing. I was really scared a lot. I got acupuncture treatments every week because doing that helped energy to release when something was trying to come to the surface. I was awake each night until 2 or 3 a.m., lying on my bed, my legs shaking with fear.

I began to feel a pull toward Sycamore Park, not far from Mamaw's house, a place I hadn't thought about in forty-five years. Mamaw lived for many years on the east side of Fort Worth, near Texas Wesleyan College. When I was eight years old, after school let out for the summer, my parents put me on a bus to go visit relatives. Both sets of grandparents lived in Fort Worth, and I would spend a week with each of them.

While I was staying with Mamaw that first year, I had a vague memory of her taking me to play miniature golf in Sycamore Park. It had been the last night of my stay with her, before I went to stay with my grandmother on Mom's side, who lived on the other side of town. I didn't remember the experience being much fun. It was a hot, muggy night in June, and I played miniature golf by myself, while Mamaw waited outside the fence.

Suddenly one weekend, I felt compelled to get in the car and drive to that park. While I drove, my stomach knotted up and I could feel my breathing getting faster, like I was running. I turned into the park, a lovely place lush with grass, a canopy of trees, and several baseball fields. It was no longer a great place to hang out – the area had gone downhill in recent years. I made sure to go in the middle of the day, when the park was completely deserted. Was it unsafe in 1958, when I was last there? I pulled off into a small parking lot, about where I thought the miniature golf course had been, now an open grassy area surrounded by trees.

I sat in the car for a moment, absorbing the sense of the place. Instinctively I looked all around, but didn't see anything or anyone unsafe. I sat there, trying to remember – something. I could mentally picture a miniature golf course, a hot, muggy June evening, and Mamaw – an odd grin of pleasure on her face. Why was all of this significant?

I got out of the car, walked over to the open grassy space, and noticed a small concrete pad, where there had been a small wooden shed to store the putters and balls. I stood on it, looking out over the grass for a long time. Nothing came to me. I began to feel uneasy and conspicuous, so I got in my car and drove home.

I went back to Sycamore Park every couple of days for about two weeks. I drove east on Berry Street, then turned north on Vaughn Boulevard, because that's how we used to get to Mamaw's house. Upon reaching Rosedale, I turned west for a short stretch, and then turned north into the park. Going that way might jog a memory, and I was willing to try anything to stir things up. I would pull into the park, check my surroundings, then sit and look at the concrete pad and the grassy area. Slowly details started to emerge, almost like snapshots, only with smells and heat and feelings.

Growing up in Northwest New Mexico we didn't have many bugs. Playing golf by myself that night, I kept getting bitten by mosquitoes, my first experience of them. I didn't have any repellant on, so they were just feeding freely. I would look down, swing at the putt, then glance nervously at my surroundings. It was hot and muggy, and I was sweaty and very uncomfortable. There was an odd, funky smell, and strange people were hanging around the park. Mamaw leaned against her car, almost impatient for me to finish, although this was supposed to be her special gift to me. I finished the game, and the memory would run dry.

I was like the amnesia patient who doesn't remember who he is, or any of his past. Yet he keeps getting glimpses, snapshot flashes – of a past he doesn't remember and didn't know existed. I would flash back to the muggy summer night, the mosquitoes, the odd unsafe presence of the strange people, and Mamaw. I sensed there was more.

While I was driving or sitting at the park, I remembered other things. We went to visit an aunt and uncle of Mamaw several times – they lived somewhere nearby. They were very unhappy people – he was bedridden, and she was taking care of him. Mamaw planted a sycamore tree in the back yard just behind the back bedroom where I stayed, and called it my tree. One of my cousins later told me she had dedicated that same tree to him. She had a white cat named Callie that wandered serenely around her house.

Mamaw's bedroom was air conditioned, but the one I stayed in wasn't. She would open all the windows and leave the back door open, with only the screen door latched. From the windows next to my bed, a huge back yard stretched into the dark night. I could hear city noises in the distance, and for a boy who had grown up in a small town, I felt very unsafe.

One time we ate hamburgers at a burger stand that sold them for twenty-five cents. Several times she took me swimming at a public pool, and sat next to the pool watching while I swam alone. Down the street from her house was a drug store, where I would get a burger, fries, and a milk shake for lunch. She left me alone at her house all day, with very little to do. She had a large lawn, and made me mow it when I stayed with her. I was really angry when I had to get out in the humid heat of June to push that mower.

A couple of times she took me where she worked, to the office of Doctor Crowder, a short, grumpy old man. He was one of the creepiest men I had ever been around – it was like he was possessed or something. When he looked at me, I was afraid to move. He didn't say much, but his eyes looked evil, and I didn't feel safe around him. He grinned at me one time, and I felt like a morsel that an alligator was surveying for dinner. Mamaw took me back into one of the examination rooms, and I could feel awful pain and suffering there. The room smelled of some stinky medicinal thing like rubbing alcohol. I couldn't wait to get out of there, and never wanted to go back. I never wanted to be around that man ever again, and could not believe my grandmother went to work with him every day.

After a couple of weeks I sensed it was time to break things loose. Little Danny, the Fear Child, was feeling more than frightened – he was now terrified, and something about going to Sycamore Park had brought it up. When I thought about that grumpy old doctor, I was filled with a dread that I could not explain.

Chapter 16: The Child Remembers More

S ome nights I wished I hadn't gone to the writer's conference, hadn't stirred things up by trying to publish a book. I lived with intense fear, which had escalated to terror. Every night my legs shook, I was so anxious I couldn't sleep, and I felt like a small scared boy late at night, lying on a bed in that hot and unsafe back bedroom at Mamaw's house. Something – some painful memory – was trying to come to the surface.

It was time for another written inner child exercise, like the one where I got Mamaw's "call you crazy and lock you up" message to the surface. I knew where I had been safe for these exercises before, so I drove to the local branch of the library, went inside, and sat at a table in the back. I sat breathing deeply for a few minutes to compose myself, and then began writing. It was July 18, 2007.

———

"Danny?"
"Yes?"
"I'd like to talk to you now."
"Okay."
"We've been releasing a lot of feelings recently, haven't we?"

"Yes, and it hasn't been much fun. But I'm not scared so much."

"That's great! I'm glad to hear it. Do you know more of the truth now?"

"Huh? I don't know what that means."

"Do you understand that it is safe for you to write. Dad won't hurt you if you do, and Mamaw won't have Doctor Crowder lock you up."

"Yeah, I know the part about Dad, but I'm not so sure about the Mamaw part."

"That's alright. Where are we now?"

"In a library."

"And you feel really safe in libraries, don't you?"

"You bet. I loved reading Lassie books at the library – it just felt good there."

"Good! Well, since you're feeling really safe, we need to dig up and let go of one more ugly message from Mamaw. Are you ready to do that?"

"Yeah, I guess so. I've been getting ready to say what happened for a while now."

"It's about Sycamore Park, isn't it? When Mamaw took you to play miniature golf?"

"Uh huh, it is."

"Alright Danny, I'm ready to hear it. Take your time and tell me what she said."

"It was that summer when she told me if I was a famous writer when I grew up, they'd call me crazy and lock me up."

"I thought it was about that time."

"She had just been going on and on about the crazy thing, all week. The next day I got to go to Big Mommy's and I was excited, because I liked being over there. I wouldn't be around Mamaw anymore, so she took me over to Sycamore Park as a treat."

"Was it fun?"

"Not so much. She sat in the car and watched me as I played putt-putt by myself."

"That couldn't have been much fun."

"It wasn't. It was hot and sticky, there were strange people around, and mosquitoes bit me."

"That doesn't sound very enjoyable. What happened next?"

"I went out of the putt-putt and Mamaw was standing by her car. She said she needed to tell me something. She had talked with Doctor Crowder, and he had told her that if she needed him to, he could have me locked up in an asylum if I went crazy from writing. She just wanted me to know that."

"How did she look?"

"She had a stern look on her face, but she also looked kind of happy."

"How did you feel?"

"I was terrified. I didn't know exactly what an asylum was, but locked up sounded horrible, and I didn't know a doctor could just do that to you. It was really scary. And that doctor was super scary. It scared me something awful to think he would be in charge of me."

"I can imagine. What happened then?"

"She told me not to talk to anyone, because people wouldn't know if I might be crazy. Only doctors could tell. I wasn't supposed to tell Big Mommy especially, because she was too fragile and might get upset."

"What did that make you feel like?"

"It felt like someone was choking me. I couldn't breathe. I really wanted to write stuff, and now it wasn't okay. I was very sad."

"What happened next?"

"We went back to her house. And after that, I don't remember. It really didn't matter anyway."

"Danny, do you understand that what she told you was not true?"

"Well sort of. It kind of doesn't make much sense."

"No, Danny, it doesn't. What Mamaw told you was a lie. There was no truth to it. Mamaw was a very sick woman, and she told you that from a very sick, mean place. Do you understand?"

"Yes, but in case I forget, will you remind me?"

"Yes, Danny. Of course I will. You just relax and know the truth. Alright?"

"Okay."

"Danny?"

"Yes?"

"I will take care of you."

"Thank you. That makes me feel good."

———

So there it was – what had happened at Sycamore Park. What a horrible thing to say to an eight-year-old child. Over the next several weeks, as I came out of shock about this revelation, a new word emerged – evil. What this woman did was nothing short of evil. Her pleased expression as she told me this awful lie was a very telling sign. Yet – all of that aside, I had to figure out how to deal with this lie, and try to move past it. It was clear that attending the writer's conference had brought this memory to the surface where it could be exposed to the light.

I had a nagging fear that I didn't want to think about, that there might be other memories yet to be remembered. Logically, moving toward publication of *Freedom's Just Another Word* would flush those old messages to the surface where they could be seen and released. It sure didn't sound like a whole lot of fun, but I had to keep pursuing it, or I would continue to strangle the writing gift I had been blessed with.

Chapter 17: The Fear and the Light

This was one of the bad nights. It was 3 a.m., and I lay on my bed on top of the covers fully dressed, with all the lights on, just in case. I couldn't concentrate so I couldn't read a book to distract myself. I had turned off the TV because I couldn't remember what I was watching. My legs had been shaking steadily for several hours. A car started in the parking lot and I went on high alert. *What was that? Was someone coming? Was something bad about to happen?* I was breathing rapidly, could feel my heart racing, but couldn't slow myself down. *How could I get away if I needed to? Where could I hide?*

Back in the '80s, I had remembered a violent incident that happened with my dad when I was a teenager. Numerous times I watched the movie *Platoon*, sitting in a darkened theater with my legs shaking as the fear released. This was worse – it felt like it was coming from a deeper place. I felt like I was being suffocated, as though I had been locked in a small room with no air. I kept gasping to catch my breath, like something heavy was pushing down on my chest, squashing me. The nebulous and terrifying image of an asylum – that undefined place Mamaw and the doctor had threatened me with – was a huge weight pressing down on me, crushing my spirit. She had made the asylum sound dark, damp, and forbidding, a place where really bad things happened, and you never got out.

The resistance I'd felt about writing, and more specifically publishing, became much more clear. It was a huge extension of my understanding, and everything made more sense. No wonder I had walked away from publishing two books. It was too dangerous to have a book out in the world. After this awareness surfaced, I purged really deep feelings all through August – I lay on the bed shaking for long periods of time.

Sometimes the fear would release as feeling memories. One time I lay on the bed and felt myself as the eight-year-old, curled up with my arms wrapped around my legs, in the back bedroom at Mamaw's house. It was the middle of June, late at night with no air conditioning, the windows open, the back door open, only the latch on a screen door to protect me. I wondered if more had happened with Mamaw, and I waited anxiously for several weeks. Nothing was revealed, and I concluded that Mamaw had said those ugly things to me about the asylum, and then must have said, "If they come for you, it will be in the middle of the night."

Night after night I would lie awake until 4 or 5 a.m., frozen and unable to sleep. My friend Karen said the bad energy she was picking up from me (she's very empathic) had kept her awake a couple of nights. She was scared to go to sleep, and it felt to her like "monsters in the closet." Mamaw had left me alone in the back bedroom of her house with my active imagination, fearing the worst.

I was eight years old when I started having nightmares. I had always thought they were from watching the movie *The Blob* with Steve McQueen, which scared me silly. For months afterward I checked under the bed before climbing in, and still couldn't sleep. Now I realized there might have been another reason. I began having nightmares, and would wake up drained, but unable to remember my dreams.

I returned to the Chinese medicine practitioner to continue acupuncture treatments, to help break things free. The fears continued to purge. I had brief moments of calm where I could set up query letters to literary agents for the memoir. With the violent incidents I had remembered about my dad, eventually the fears subsided, and I thought it would happen in a similar way this time. That was tough to remember when I was lying on my bed at 3 a.m., with my legs shaking.

As I lay on the table during one acupuncture session, I assured Danny, the eight-year-old boy I had been, that the things Mamaw had told us were lies, that he could be safe, and that I understood it was painful to let these old fears out. I told him that on the other side was great joy. I could sense him take heart from these words, but he was still afraid of the monsters that might get him. Again the phrase "monsters in the closet" pulsed through me. Why monsters, and what was this about a closet?

At the next acupuncture session, I unexpectedly visualized Danny in the back room at Mamaw's house in the dark, in the middle of the night, and not feeling safe. Suddenly I visualized a bright light, which encircled him and formed an impenetrable barrier. The light exposed the entire bedroom, so there were no hidden corners where monsters could hide. Danny felt safe and protected. I hadn't felt this safe since I was very young. It was phenomenal, and a very healing experience. It took a couple of days to realize the power of visualizing that bright light, and the protection it provided.

I became more and more convinced that the light barrier exposing the corners of the darkened room had given Danny safety, and that the effect of Mamaw's cruel words had been broken. Was it true, or just wishful thinking?

By the end of August, I relaxed enough to get some rest. The fear released with diminishing magnitude like a wave coming up on the beach just before it dies out. I tentatively accepted that I was, at long last, free to spring into action, like Chuck Yeager attacking the sound barrier. That would prove true, but I forgot – there was some turbulence when he broke the sound barrier, powerful resistance to push through.

Chapter 18: Breaking Through The Block

I t's an interesting experience to think about reading words you wrote almost two years ago and haven't looked at since. I had begun writing *Freedom's Just Another Word* during the Christmas holidays in 2005, and now it was the holiday season in 2007. I was almost ready to see the result of my efforts.

I had felt very inspired while writing the manuscript, and I think it was because of the writing method I used. I once read C. S. Forester's description of his process in writing the *Horatio Hornblower* series of nautical adventure books. He would gather research materials, and then study them intensively. The basic information would submerge below the conscious surface, and gather like barnacles on the keel of a ship, while he went on about his daily life. After a time those pieces would rise to the surface and cling together very coherently, to provide him the text of the next part he needed to write. Reading that was great comfort, because I heard a lot about how writers should be writing on a daily basis, and that had never worked for me.

In my writing process, I first would read journal entries about the section I was about to write, then jot a few notes about how the elements of the next chapter might link together. I would return to my daily life, working, running, not thinking about writing. After about a week of letting things percolate below the surface, I would sit down to write. Many times it happened on a Sunday afternoon, after I had unwound from the workweek. Elements began to gather and flow together, and I wrote with an easy flow. Chapters would emerge fully realized. During that time I had relocated from New Mexico to Texas, and made several job changes. In spite of all of that, I maintained a consistent writing voice from chapter to chapter. It was quite astonishing how the story unfolded so clearly and easily. Finally, I felt ready to see what I had written.

———

One day I called Karen. "Hey there, it's me. How are things going?"

"Great here, how are you doing? You sound a little tense."

"Yeah, I guess maybe I am. I think I'm ready to read the first draft."

"I thought you might be getting close. Do you want any feedback?"

"Maybe just the big picture."

"Sure. First, the structure of the story is solid all the way from beginning to end."

"Awesome. That was one of my big worries."

"I know. The story is tight, and will need minimal cleanup. You'll see what needs editing."

"How about the voice? Was that part good?"

"Very much so. The voice is very consistent all the way through."

"Excellent. Thanks for telling me all of this. If you would, please email me the file."

The next day I sat down for the first time and read the manuscript all the way through. Passages that needed editing were easy to spot. Many times I would leave a thought incomplete – I knew what I meant, but forgot to add the details. I didn't edit, because I just wanted to see how the overall story affected me. I noted rough spots and moved on.

The way I had combined elements felt intuitively solid and very creative. I would take something happening in real time, then connect it to an event in the past, and make the current event more palpable and real. Combining the present with past events really illuminated my healing process. It was a solid piece of writing, and I could only shake my head in amazement at the way the topic had been developed. I could see the whole manuscript very objectively, and letting the manuscript get really cold before reading it was paying off.

It was clear that I was in a different emotional space from my previous writing attempts. Before, I had tried to write without any knowledge of the deep wounds that

Mamaw had inflicted on me. I had been blocked from seeing how well I could write, from owning that talent, and from appreciating it or finding joy in the process. I was convinced all the incidents where she had said damaging things to me had been revealed. I had released a lot of the feelings from those old events. I was left with a freedom to accept my writing gift more comfortably. I remembered how I had sidestepped when my friends would try to point out my writing gift, and how I had pushed away efforts from so many people to help me let that talent loose. Knowing about the damage by Mamaw, it made perfect sense why I had resisted so much.

Reading the manuscript only confirmed the need to pursue my writing. I had to break this writer's block – or publishing block – completely, and share my writing with those who would be interested and who might benefit.

———

It was time to get more feedback on the manuscript. At times I will discount what I hear from someone who knows me really well, and I sometimes did that with Karen. I needed to get another opinion, to reinforce Karen's feedback.

I asked my friend Scott to read the manuscript, because I needed an outsider's opinion – someone who didn't know as much background as some of my other friends. I had known Scott for a number of years; he was highly intelligent and worked in the Information Technology field, but was very intuitive and spiritually in tune with himself. Scott had a great way of getting down to the heart of a matter and speaking his truth clearly, which I really wanted to hear. He was thrilled and honored to be asked, and said he would start reading that weekend, so I emailed a digital copy of the manuscript to him.

He called me the next night. "Dan, your book is really amazing! I just couldn't stop reading it."

I tried to let the words sink in. He said he was blown away, and kept referring to it as a contemplative meditation. He didn't read much nonfiction, had read few memoirs, and didn't know what to expect. He quickly got into the rhythm of the story and became totally engrossed and overwhelmed.

"Dan, I'm not sure exactly how to describe what is so powerful about your writing. I'm a computer guy. Hey, what do I know about writing styles? But reading your words has gotten to me in a really deep and powerful way. Granted, I've only read about the first thirty pages. I was going to print it all out and then read it this weekend. But then I started reading as the pages came off the printer, and couldn't stop. I was plunged into your story so quickly it was incredible. The way you describe your meeting with that Wayne guy – even down to walking into his office through that funky door that looked like it was out of a pirate ship or something.

It was all just so real – I could feel it. And when he put you down with his harsh words, and you got angry after that, it was just incredible."

"Scott, this is wonderful feedback. I really hear what you're saying. What's amazing is that the first thirty pages is just the setup. The book really starts to heat up at about that point, and the real rollercoaster ride begins."

"If that's the case, I can't wait. And I'm thinking that if the early part of the manuscript can bring up this strong a response, the reader will trust the writer more, and from feeling that initial power, know that more is coming, and want to read on." I sat with that thought.

.

Part Four

Down To The Roots

Chapter 19: A Writer's Road Trip

After all the recovery work I had done, I was depleted, and needed a break. It was time for spiritual renewal, to recharge my system – for me that meant a trip to New Mexico. Specifically Farmington. What was the pull, and why was it so strong? I had asked myself that question many times over the years. Farmington was a small town of about thirty thousand tucked in to the northwest corner of the state, not far from the famous Four Corners – the only spot in the Continental U.S. where four states came together.

The town was in the middle of the Navajo reservation, and had a strong Indian cultural influence. There was a special energy about the whole area – I'd even read that it was a spiritual power spot similar to Sedona in Arizona. I found that easy to believe, because I felt creatively alive, yet very grounded, during visits there. It was a very safe place, and the site of some of my most productive writing work.

I grew up in Farmington – attending school from first grade until we moved in the middle of my junior year in high school. In the late '50s and early '60s it was a small town that felt very safe and protected. We left our cars parked on the street with the keys in them, and no one ever thought about it. I never remember our house being locked. There was quite a buzz when they added a fifth digit on our phone numbers.

I was very active in school, especially in junior high – we had speech contests, published a literary magazine called *Scholarly Scribbles*, and I was on the annual staff. When we weren't in class, there were miles of canyons and deserts to explore. My dad and I went fishing at Jackson's Lake, and though we seldom caught many fish, had a pleasant time together. I grew up able to see the huge monolith of Shiprock off in the distance to the west, and woke up invigorated by crisp mornings and moderate weather. I felt a warm energy around Farmington, in spite of the unhappy memories when I was a teenager, as my parents' drinking escalated.

On the way to Farmington, I wanted to stop over in Albuquerque, where I had lived from 2002 to 2006, and go to an ACA twelve-step meeting I had attended. I would have lunch with friends, then drive to Farmington and spend some time editing the book. The next Friday I would drive back south to Albuquerque, go to the meeting once more, and then return to Fort Worth. I liked the plan. I thought it was a rest break and a way of connecting with a spiritual anchor. Little did I know I'd get more incredible feedback about the book I had just written.

I drove in to Albuquerque, checked into a motel, and spent a relaxing evening. As I stepped out of the Owl Café after a great enchilada dinner, I breathed deeply and enjoyed the clear night sky and chilly weather. Saturday morning I checked out of the motel and drove to the ACA meeting, and visited with several old friends. I shared in the meeting about how my creativity had blossomed, and that I was about to publish a book.

I gave a man named William a copy of my book, to hear his feedback when he had time to read it. A woman named Deborah expressed quite an interest in the book. She had heard about it from William, so I told him I was fine with letting her read it. The group went out to lunch and it was great to visit with everyone. One woman had come down from Santa Fe just to see me, because one of the leaders had announced in the meeting I was coming to town. I was really touched by that. People were very interested in how my writing had progressed, and it was a very enjoyable experience. I was very heartened by the warm reception I got.

After lunch, I drove to Farmington, enjoying the red-tinged bluffs and mesas, the expanding horizon, the sandy slopes of Huerfano Mesa off to my right, the blue outlines of mountains to the far north. I drove down into the river valley, through Bloomfield and into Farmington. I relaxed. I checked in to my favorite motel, which had more personality than just a box with a bathroom. It was very quaint, with '50s tile in the bathroom, a huge bathtub, and wooden closets and accessories. I liked staying there.

I got out and drove around town, exploring the place I still considered my home base. I cruised down Twentieth Street past the high school – where I'd been in Honors English class, and we put on a performance of the Greek play Medea. I drove by Hermosa Middle School, the source of so many of my warm memories, from the annual staff to being manager for the sports teams. I meandered out Main Street and drove up to San Juan Country Club, where I learned to swim and play golf. I drove past our house on Crescent Street, and frowned a bit – by the time we moved there, the memories had begun to grow painful.

I settled in to a comfort zone, and could feel myself unwind. I felt safe enough to be really creative in this small town. Later, my safety zone would expand, and I could be creative and write almost anywhere, but for right now, it was good to be back and connect with the energy of Farmington. I had a sense I might learn something while I was here, but had no idea how creatively empowering my week would be.

Chapter 20: A Time of Inspiration

S unday night at the motel, I called a friend in Albuquerque, who commented that Mamaw had put a heavy burden of negative weight on my creativity, which had caused me a lot of damage. I began to reflect on the creativity issue. I would need to write about that whole experience, but had planned to do it many years later, after writing several other books. My reasoning was that I had only begun to remember those events in 2003, and would address other events first.

I called Karen Monday morning to check in, and at one point she asked, for about the third time, when I was going to write the book about my grandmother. She thought that if I wrote about later events without first explaining what happened with Mamaw, readers would be puzzled about the "I may be crazy" comments which floated around in my head so often (much as I had been puzzled at the time of those events). In her mind it made sense to go ahead and describe what happened with Mamaw, because it was a critical part of my healing journey. I saw the logic of it. She had given me a gentle nudge in a direction that intuitively felt right. The idea of making that the next book I would write picked up momentum.

Dan L. Hays

I drove to the Farmington library on Tuesday to flesh out a few thoughts on paper. As I walked into the building, I realized it was in this library that I had written the inner child exercise to uncover the message about "They'll call you crazy and lock you up." I walked through the book stacks and sat down with a pen and legal pad, at the same table I had used before. It was odd to return, about to conceptualize the book that would expose my grandmother's lies to the light.

I began to jot down notes. I wrote with confidence and clarity, and the important components of the book that would later become *Healing The Writer* began to coalesce on paper.

Where would this story begin? It had to start the day I received the phone call from the publisher in 1986, when he was excited about publishing *Search For Peace*. Why was my response fear instead of elation? I wrote it down:

I sent the book to several ACA publishers. I sent it to Claudia Black's publishing company. Four days later, Jack Fahey called. He was Claudia Black's husband, and her business manager. He raved about the book, even quoting passages of it to me. It freaked me out, and I didn't follow up with him.

The wheat harvest novel was an essential element. It would be a brief segment – the significance of that manuscript for this current memoir was that I had walked away from it, and abandoned a second book.

In 1991 and 1992 I went on the wheat harvest to research a book about my dad, and what had happened that changed his life, made him sober up and start recovery. I wrote the book over the next two years, and in 1994, I sent query letters out to agents for the manuscript of Nothing Left To Lose.

The time at Denny's when I asked Joe Vitale, the marketing expert, to help me draft a query letter was pivotal. He had brought up the terribly significant question that I could not answer.

I paid Joe Vitale to help me draft the query letter, and as we were discussing it, Search For Peace *came up. I told him how I had stopped pursuing publication of the book. He looked at me curiously, and asked, "How are you going to make sure it doesn't happen again?" I stumblingly commented that I was in a different place now, but I really didn't have a good answer.*

The inner child exercise – which I had done in this library, at this very table, was key to unlocking the mystery of my writer's block.

In 2003, I felt like something was coming up. I went to the Farmington library, and Little Danny remembered about Mamaw. She was my dad's mother, and when we lived in Farmington, I rode a bus to Fort Worth when I was eight years old, to visit relatives. I stayed with Mamaw for about a week. She asked what I wanted to be when I grew up. I told her I wanted to be a famous writer. She said oh no, I didn't want to do that. I asked her why, and she said, "If you're a famous writer they will call you crazy and lock you up." I wrote the incident, but didn't really process it, and forgot about it for a couple of years.

As I continued to write I could sense something special happening. I felt confident – about my talent as a writer and how to exercise my craft. I wrote rapidly to capture thoughts on paper, but with a sure hand, a clear vision – and no uncertainty. Thoughts gathered into scenes, scenes collected into chapters, each chapter leading to the next without hesitation.

It was a wonderful and invigorating experience; the instant where a set of life experiences gathered themselves into a book – the next book I would write. That brief time in the library transcended all my previous attempts at writing. I remembered that before, I had to reflect for a long time before putting words on paper, but this experience felt completely different. I wrote freely and with a quick certainty, something which had never happened before. What emerged was a fully realized vision for a book. It felt glorious.

I would take great delight in writing that book – a joyful story of healing, of the reclamation of a writer's talent. It was a story of leading my writing gift from the chains of a deep darkness to the light of day where the product of my pen could be shared with the world. I sat for a while at the table and just looked at my notes, terribly excited by the joy of the experience. I was energized. I was empowered.

It was like that crisp fall night when I was in my thirties. Our men's team was playing softball and I was at bat. I hit a screaming line drive just out of reach of the shortstop; as I sprinted around first base and headed for second, I saw the outfielders frantically chasing the ball toward the fence; I had the footspeed and decided to push on, made the turn at second, dug deep around third base, flew across home plate standing up, with a big smile and a whooping yell at my "in the park" home run, joyfully alive with the thrill of having done something exceptionally well.

Now I felt the same thrill. I was astonished by the comprehensive vision of the next book I would write and how quickly it had emerged. I smiled and gave a quiet fist pump, forsaking the yell since I was in a library.

Then I did savor the moment.

Chapter 21: The Landscape of a Writer

I needed to absorb the amazing session of creative clarity that I had just enjoyed. It felt like I had gone a long way in a short time, and needed to let the experience settle in where I could appreciate it fully. The next day I got up and drove out to Shiprock, the monolith to the west of Farmington. It was a real energy source and an anchor for me, a volcanic plug seventeen hundred feet high, rising out of the flat desert floor, and one of the sacred mountains for the Navajo tribe. A mystical energy surrounded that spire.

A drive out to Shiprock had become a ritual on trips to Farmington. I drove west through the small town also named Shiprock, took the highway south toward Gallup. I turned west on a secondary road, drove a few miles west until the monolith was to my north. It was inaccessible from the highway, so I pulled onto a driveway leading to a gate, which got me completely off the road. I got out of the car. I stood and absorbed the power of the massive rock, not thinking much, hearing the silence of the wide open spaces, only occasionally broken by the passage of a car. I drew spiritual strength from being so close to such a sacred space.

Next, I drove north toward Durango and pulled in to the Ute Mountain Casino. My trip to Farmington had been hugely successful, and it was time to just relax and sightsee. I played blackjack for several hours – I broke even. Then the noise and visual overload of the casino began to drain me, and I drove back to the motel in Farmington.

For the next couple of days I drove around Farmington. Everywhere I looked brought up memories. The empty field where we played army was now a subdivision. The lonely canyon we explored had houses all around the top of it, and didn't feel like our hidden fortress any more. In a small-town tradition, there was a large "F" on a distant bluff that overlooked the football stadium. In the '60s the sophomores climbed up and whitewashed it before homecoming. It was surrounded by houses, and had a small park at its base. There were changes everywhere – signs of my childhood world disappearing.

I had spent many hours swimming each summer at Brookside Park on North Dustin, just south of Twentieth Street. The pool had been completely remodeled, and there was a new skate park next to it. When I was about ten my dad would pile the family in the station wagon and drive up to the airport, which sat on top of a bluff. There were no fences, so we parked near the edge of the runway, and watched as airplanes took off and landed. Now the whole area was fenced off and inaccessible.

I drove down Main Street – in the 1950s the short strip of downtown was a hub of our world. The Allen and Totah theaters were about a block apart on opposite sides of the street. Moms would drop us off on Saturday morning, to watch cowboy movies and Looney Tunes cartoons. It saddened me to see both theaters closed and abandoned, eclipsed by the multiplex at the mall. On Saturday nights the high school kids would drag Main Street from the A & W Root Beer stand on the east, to the Tastee Freeze on the west end. Now those hangouts were gone, and the kids were out at the mall.

I drove far up into the hills and parked on top of a bluff. The clear blue sky felt limitless, with only a few clouds in sight. Not far west was a formation called the Hogback – a rocky geological upthrust hundreds of feet high that ran like a spine for miles. Further west and south was the volcanic peak of Shiprock. South across the sprawling town, houses and subdivisions covered hills and flat spaces in a jumbled and random pattern. Thin bands of cottonwood trees defined the line of the river – actually three rivers which intersected. Tall sandy-colored bluffs walled the far side of the valley. Beyond those bluffs lay endless miles of desert, along with the bizarre rock formations of the Bisti Wilderness and the extensive ruins of Chaco Canyon.

To the southeast was the lonely spire of Angel Peak, and just below the horizon was Huerfano Mesa, a sacred spot in the Navajo

Indian mythology. To the east were the great kivas of the pueblo ruins in the town of Aztec. I turned north to look out over miles of desert, sprinkled with scattered dark green pinon trees. Sixty miles away, low and blue on the horizon were the La Plata Mountains, including Hesperus Peak, one of the sacred mountains of the Navajos. To the northwest the famous cliff dwellings of Mesa Verde were tucked up in the mountains.

I had never stopped to think about it before, but the number of powerful locations surrounding Farmington was astonishing. I drew strength from all of it, and saw more clearly why there was such a special energy to this small town. I breathed deeply as I looked across the powerful and open vistas. In a similar way, my writing horizons had expanded in a larger and more positive direction. I felt different – empowered, with an increased clarity about my writing, a tremendous ease with being creative, and my destiny as a writer. I relaxed into the awareness.

There was a forecast of snow for Friday morning in Farmington, so I left early to avoid possibly getting trapped by a heavy snowfall. With an extra day in Albuquerque, it was fun to explore some of my old haunts. I browsed around several used bookstores on Central Avenue, and found several old *Hardy Boys* books that brought up fond memories from my childhood. In the evening, I drove out to a basketball game at Cibola High School, to watch a team that had been a powerhouse while I lived there. There were several people I knew in the stands, but the team wasn't doing that well, and the game was poorly attended. It was disappointing.

Saturday morning I drove over to the ACA meeting. When I walked into the room Deborah came up and began to talk excitedly. William had given her his copy of the manuscript, and thinking she had to finish it this week, she had read the whole thing.

"Dan, your book has really opened my eyes – I'm just astonished at how much of your own journey you shared! You took me places that I knew I needed to go, but I didn't know how to get there. I feel like now I know!" She shared in the meeting about the book she had just read that had really expanded her thinking. Hearing the impact of my manuscript was pretty powerful, and I just tried to absorb her words.

After the meeting, William tried to give me back the manuscript copy I had given him, and I and told him it was his to keep. He was amazed that I would do that, and said, "It's like you've given me a road map for how to get past the abuse." Someone else asked when he could read it. I suggested he ask William, who gave him the book. The impact the book had on people was tangible. We went to lunch again, and had a very nice visit. People were focused on what I was doing and how my creativity had exploded, and I was touched by all the interest.

I had just gotten a lot of affirmation for being a writer, and some powerful feedback about *Freedom's Just Another Word*. It was time to go home. The next morning I drove back to Fort Worth, tired, but spiritually refreshed and renewed. I was also creatively empowered and liked the feeling. The whole trip felt like a huge positive. Now it was time to face the part that had tripped me up before – publication.

Chapter 22: Seeking Publication Again

I was pretty uneasy about approaching publication again, because it took a lot of work to write a book, only to abandon it. I wondered if I might "lock up" and walk away from a book for a third time. I just knew I had to try – I had to give it my best shot.

I wanted to let *Freedom's Just Another Word* get cold before reviewing it again. I used the time to check out publication options. The writer's conference had given me a much more current idea of what was happening in the publishing industry, and I quickly compiled a list of literary agents who might want to represent the book I had written. I chose the fifteen strongest possibilities for my first round of submissions, and set the rest aside for later if needed.

If a literary agent accepted the manuscript, and that agent secured a publishing contract with a traditional publisher, I wanted to have the contract reviewed by a lawyer. One of the breakout sessions at the writer's conference the previous summer dealt with the publishing contract. While the literary agent represented the author, they were not always proficient in evaluating contracts, so the author had to make sure he was conversant with the contract he was offered. I had worked extensively with legal documents in the oil and gas industry, and was very aware of the prudence of engaging a professional to review a contract.

A lawyer friend in the oil and gas industry volunteered to review the literary contract, but that didn't really work for me. His specialty was real estate, so it would be like having a heart specialist evaluate a brain problem. I found two lawyers in New York City with solid credentials in the publishing industry, in case I needed them.

From my research, submitting queries was still the same. I worked from the query for the novel *Nothing Left To Lose*, and wrote what felt like a strong letter for the current book. I printed out query letters for the top fifteen agents, and dropped them in the mail. I was excited and nervous about what I had just done, and went about my daily life while I waited for the results.

The query letter I sent out for *Freedom's Just Another Word* started with themes familiar to publishers, because they had been written about so often – a death in the family combined with alcoholism. Looking back, I realized that the negative messages from Mamaw intruded, and I sabotaged myself unconsciously. I couldn't see that at the time. Instead of emphasizing positive aspects that made this manuscript different from other books with those themes, I had put a negative spin on the query letter, and most likely influenced literary agents against what I had written.

My friend Karen later reminded me that she had strongly recommended I not use the first sentence of the query, but I thought it worked well, and wouldn't budge. The query began:

"An alcoholic father's death leads a middle aged man to a startling revelation, healing, and the seeds of forgiveness. *Freedom's Just Another Word* is a 55,000-word memoir, set in Houston, Texas, in 1987."

By the time ten replies came in declining the book, I accepted the fact that there wasn't going to be a request for my manuscript. I was crushed, but tried to push down the feelings because it hurt so badly. I had a number of other agents on my list, but I had already submitted to the strongest possibilities, so there was a likelihood of more "No thank you" replies. I was so deflated that I couldn't face the possibility of further rejections, so I stopped sending queries.

With *Search For Peace*, the autobiography I had written in 1985, when a publisher was very interested – I walked away. Several agents were interested in the novel *Nothing Left To Lose* – and I walked away again. With *Freedom's Just Another Word*, I had minimized my chances of publication with the first sentence of the query letter. At the time, I didn't see that the Mamaw message about being a famous writer and "called crazy and locked up" was underneath this repeated pattern.

———

I was really hurt and disappointed at the rejections, but after a couple of weeks, realized I had to move forward. I didn't want to walk away from publication for a third time. I felt powerless to overcome whatever was getting in my way, but I had to keep trying.

I checked out self-publishing again, which still had the aura of "vanity publishing," when publishers agreed to print books for an author, who paid all production expenses. Books were published with little attention to quality, and got a bad reputation. Traditional reviewers like *Publishers Weekly* wouldn't even consider reviewing a self-published book. Even with the limitations, I still wanted to investigate the possibility. There was a huge difference between self-publishing in 1994 and the current process in 2008. The self-publishing industry had undergone a radical change, brought about by digital publishing, known as Print On Demand (POD). Now, digital files were stored at a warehousing facility, and a book was only printed when a copy was ordered, which made the cost of publication minimal.

Self-publishing had some definite advantages – the author was not controlled by the publisher's print schedule, and could put the book on the market more quickly. Traditional publishers were currently not offering much support with publicity, which lessened their advantage over self-publishing. The author had to generate most of his own publicity under either alternative.

This alternative to traditional publishing looked interesting. I contacted a Print On Demand publisher, and their publication cycle was approximately four months. That was too soon for me – I wasn't that close to finishing the book. I wasn't sure about publishing in the summer, when the presidential election conventions would deflect interest from other issues like the publication of books. The fall didn't look much better, with the election coming in November.

I decided to target January 2009 to self-publish my book, which would clear all the election news and allow me plenty of time to finish the manuscript and get publicity outlets lined up. It felt like a solid plan and evolved very quickly. (Was I stalling with the distant publication goal? It sure looked like it.)

Karen mentioned that she was still at work checking the editing changes I had made to the manuscript, and had a feeling I would need a well-revised copy sooner than next fall – she wanted to have it available for me by June. I didn't know exactly what that meant, but it confirmed the sense that I needed to keep pushing forward toward publication.

Chapter 23: Dark Fear Rises

My commitment to move toward publication forced something closer to the surface, and more feelings began to release. I drove by Mamaw's old house, to visualize what it looked like inside, something I hadn't done for a while. I came home and drew up a floor plan of the house, and spent a long time picturing the layout and how the rooms fit together.

I did weekly acupuncture sessions because they always broke abuse energy free for me. The week of April 14th was the deepest and most all-consuming fear I had ever released on my healing journey. I felt paralyzed and unable to move. I couldn't look at the floor plan I had drawn of Mamaw's house, nor could I read the synopsis I had written for the book about her.

During that week I felt myself being inside that house. *"Someone help me. Get me out of here. I'm scared!"* Once again I felt like that eight-year-old boy, alone in that back bedroom, late at night in the dangerous city. I was unsafe, unprotected, and terrified. It felt like there was no air – I couldn't catch my breath. The room felt dark, even with all the lights on. I smelled dust, and there was something about shoes. I lay on my bed, my heart racing, shivering like I was in a meat locker. My legs shook violently, and I wanted to run away. I was breathing rapidly, and my heart rate wouldn't slow down. I felt very unsafe, and I had a terrible sense of doom – something awful, like death, was about to happen, and there was no way to stop it. I listened intently to any noises around me, and tried to hold my breath, as if that would make it go away. My legs shook horribly; I'm not sure how long it went on each night – it felt like forever. I went deeper into the memory than ever before, and felt it on a much more visceral level. It was awful.

I began to sense that Mamaw had either locked me in the closet to show me what an asylum would feel like, or that she had threatened me with it. I couldn't tell which it was, but I could feel it deep in my gut. It heightened what Karen had picked up on last summer, that I had little boy energy and that there were "monsters in the closet." It always came back to the closet in the back bedroom in Mamaw's house on Hazeline Street in East Fort Worth.

I remembered a History Channel show on TV one evening, about the underground world beneath Edinburgh, Scotland. The new town had been built on top of the old, which left a maze of streets and passageways underground. Slavers kidnapped women off the streets to force them into prostitution and white slavery. They would lock a kidnapped woman in a small box about the size of an outhouse for several days, in total darkness, to subdue her. After that period of isolation, the woman would be completely tamed and obedient. I had been terrified watching that, and on some deep level, I understood what that total blackness and total aloneness felt like. Mamaw had threatened me with a scary dark place called an asylum, and it horrified me to hear about something similar.

I reread the inner child exercises I had written, to revisit what had happened with Mamaw. After miniature golf at Sycamore Park where she told me "I can have you committed to an asylum," I was struck by the way Little Danny concluded, "We went back to her house. And after that, I don't remember. It really didn't matter anyway." It sure sounded like "I don't want to remember."

I mentally dialogued with Danny, to let him know that it was time to release whatever was going on right now – I wanted him to consider telling me what else had happened. I didn't want to force him, but we needed to get this resolved or it would stop the publication process yet again. If we released whatever else he remembered, it would lead to great joy and I would be able to write more freely.

I emotionally prepared for a trip to the library – the safe place – to write a Gestalt dialogue with Danny, to see if he would tell me what he was still so fearful about. It was scary to even think about. I was clear that I couldn't rush the process and force Little

Danny to open up to me, but that I needed to respect him and let him get ready in his own time. Gentleness was the key at that point.

———————

One night I met for dinner with my long time friend Gregg, the third man Randy and I used to meet with back in the early '90s, before I went on the wheat harvest. He had moved to Fort Worth, and we got together for dinner. I told him what had come up for me with the Mamaw stuff.

"You know, Gregg, I can't tell if she really locked me in the closet or just threatened to. That part is still vague."

Gregg said, "I'm not sure if it really matters. She planted the seed of that abuse, and you were left carrying the fear, subconsciously, that you would be locked up if you became a successful author. If you were eight years old, your mind wouldn't know the difference at that point. It would have felt so real, it was like it really happened." I thought about it for a minute, and had to agree.

Gregg continued. "I find it really conspicuous that first your dad, and at a much deeper level Mamaw, both attacked your writing. That was a specific point of their abuse." The thought was astonishing. Now maybe I had a reason why he had kept his dream of being a writer secret for so many years — very possibly Mamaw attacked him over his writing like she did to me. As a result, two people attacked me over my writing very systematically. I mulled that over.

"I don't know if you've noticed," Gregg said, "but you've used the exact words 'locked up' a number of times with respect to your writing. You'll say things like, 'I feel locked up creatively,' 'things feel locked up emotionally,' 'I'll start to move forward and things will just lock up.' I think that is terribly profound, as if your subconscious has been trying to tell you something. Think about it. If you were in that bedroom late at night looking at the closet door, which wasn't safe; the door to the rest of the house where Mamaw was, which wasn't safe; the door to the back porch, which wasn't safe – how could you feel any safety in that situation? It was like you were already locked up." I thought about the awareness he had shared for a long time. Sitting in that back bedroom, I had experienced that deep, dank asylum place in a very emotionally tangible way.

It was odd that Mamaw had asked me "What do you want to be?" almost as soon as I got off the bus to visit her in Fort Worth. I wondered if maybe Dad had mentioned something about how bright and gifted I was, maybe said something about writing, and gave her the ammunition she needed. I would never know for sure. My nightmares started when I was eight years old – I began to suspect it was connected to the events with Mamaw. The talk with Gregg had opened my eyes to a number of things I had not seen before. I felt ready – it was time to do another inner child exercise and find out what else had happened.

Chapter 24: How My Writing Got Locked Up

On a Thursday when I woke up, I knew it was time – I was ready for the written inner child exercise. I went to the Fort Worth Library, sat down at a table in the back of the book stacks, and composed myself. After a few deep breaths, I began to write. The rest of the incident with Mamaw came out, and it was chilling. Once again I was talking to a terrified eight-year-old child:

"Danny?"

"Yes?"

"I'd like to talk to you. You know, about what else happened with Mamaw. Are you ready to tell me what happened?"

"Uh ... I guess so."

"Danny, I know this will be painful for you. It's not going to be a pleasant memory, I can already sense that."

"It makes my stomach hurt."

"I can imagine. Remember what I've told you before – that talking about these old ugly things helps them go away so you can be free to feel the joy of writing? You want to do that, don't you?"

"Sure, that part sounds good."

"I understand. It's time to let go of more of Mamaw's lies."

"But that just makes it more scary."

"Because all the things Mamaw told you get closer to happening?"

"Well yeah, if people read the writing, they might like it, and there might be the famous thing, and then, you know."

"What? Tell me again."

"They would call me crazy and lock me up."

"But those were all lies – remember us talking about that?"

"It's hard to remember it. She said the other stuff so much. Will you remind me?"

"Of course I will. We will just keep working to let you see that what she said was all lies, and won't happen. Alright?"

"Yeah, okay."

"Are you ready to talk about what else happened?"

"I guess so. You promise I won't get hurt if I tell?"

"No, you won't get hurt. Do you remember the Dracula movies?"

"For sure, they were super scary."

"Well, you remember how Dracula could never go out in the sunlight? If he did he would wither up and die?"

"Oh yeah, that part was really cool."

"Well, if we expose Mamaw's lies to the light they will wither up and die. They won't hurt you anymore. And she will not have power over you anymore."

"That sounds really neat!"

"It will be. Now, let's talk about when Mamaw took you to Sycamore Park, to play miniature golf."

"I think I might throw up."

"I understand. But that will only be for a little while, and we can be free of this. So Mamaw told you Dr. Crowder could have you put in an asylum, right?"

"Yeah, I didn't know what an asylum was, but it sounded pretty bad. No way I was going to ask what it was."

"Something else happened that night, didn't it?"

"Yes."

"Can you tell me?"

"Okay. We drove home, and Mamaw was all happy and giggly. Until she started talking about taking me over to Grandmother Justin's the next day. Then she looked a little sad, and a lot angry."

"Why do you think that was?"

"She said she didn't like them over there because they thought they were better than her. She didn't like them a lot. We got home and she asked if I really understood about what Doctor Crowder could do to me. I wasn't sure why she kept talking about it, or what she wanted me to say. So I just kind of nodded, and said 'Uh huh.' I guess she didn't like that. She said she needed to show me what it would be like in an asylum. She had been inside one before as a nurse, and she knew what they were like."

"What was she like right then?"

"She was smiling but she had kind of a really creepy look on her face. Twisted like."

"So what did she do?"

"She took me in the back bedroom, where I stayed, and opened the closet door. She said they would lock me up in a room about that big and leave me in there for a long time. And if they did, the doctor said sometimes they just left you in there and you died in the dark."

"How did it feel when she showed you this?"

"It felt awful – it sounded real scary to be closed up like that, with the dark and dying and all."

"What happened next?"

"She said I needed to know what it felt like, so she told me to go in the closet for a while."

"That must have sounded awful."

"Yeah, I thought she might just leave me. I felt really cold, and my stomach hurt more. I told her I didn't want to do that."

"What did she say?"

"She said if I didn't do what she wanted, she would call Doctor Crowder right then, and he would take me to be locked up in an asylum for a couple of days, just to show me what it was like. She said doing this wouldn't be nearly as bad. And she was doing it for my own good."

"So what did you do?"

"When she talked about that creepy old doctor, there was no way I wanted him taking me away. I never wanted to be around him ever again. So I went into the closet, and she closed the door behind me."

"What happened then?"

"I was standing there and heard a click, and it got really dark."

"What did you do then?"

"I pushed some shoes where I could sit down in the corner, with my arms around my legs. I couldn't understand why she was doing this. My stomach hurt really bad, but I couldn't open the door or it would get worse. So I just sat."

"Was it quiet?"

"No, I could hear the TV in Mamaw's room, and sometimes she would laugh."

"How long were you in there?"

"I don't know, it felt like forever. I guess it was until her bedtime. She opened the door and the light was real bright. She told me I could come out now, and it was time to go to bed. She said she hoped I had learned the lesson – not to ever be a famous writer, or really bad things would happen. I just nodded, and she left."

"What did you do then?"

"I got in bed, but I couldn't sleep."

"Yes, I can imagine. What was going on for you?"

"Well, I kept thinking about that closet door – I couldn't see it in the dark, but I kind of could see it in my mind still. It was real scary. So I just sat on the bed with my arms wrapped around my legs, looking around and listening. I was really scared she'd change her mind and call that creepy doctor and he'd come for me. I knew if that happened, I might die."

"Wow, Danny, you must have been really frightened."

"Oh yeah, it was so super scary. I was sick to my stomach."

"Could you go to sleep?"

"I guess I did, after a long time."

"Danny, that was a horrible thing to happen to you, and I'm sorry you had to go through it. You've been very brave to tell me about it. Thank you."

"Okay. You're really sure I'm safe?"

"Yes Danny, you are safe. There was never any truth to any of the things she told you. Her putting you in the closet was horrible, and a very bad thing. But do you see how sick she was, to do something like that to a bright, gifted eight-year-old child?"

"Kind of."

"You've exposed her craziness to the light now, and it can start withering up and dying now, and you can be free of it."

"Like Dracula."

"Exactly. You've been very brave to come out and tell me this. Remember - this will lead to great joy and freedom – and safety. And that's why we've been doing it. How do you feel Danny?"

"I feel better. A lot better. And my stomach doesn't hurt anymore."

"Great, Danny! Glad to hear it. Now go rest. You deserve it!"

I sat at the library table for a few minutes to gather myself, and then I had to get out of there. I could barely drive home because I felt so shaky, but I had to find a safe place.

Mamaw had made an asylum sound like a dungeon, and I knew with vivid horror what that meant. I saw the movie *Ben Hur* not long after being put in the closet. At one point Ben Hur's mother and sister are falsely imprisoned, and he comes back several years later to free them. The dungeon boss says, "Yes, I think they're still in there." The jailer goes down into the bowels of the dungeon, walls slimy with scum, water on the floors, dank and cold, where it's obvious that if he didn't have a torch, it would be pitch black. He says, "I know they're still alive, because they keep taking the food plate." So they've been thrown into total darkness and forgotten.

According to the doctor, if I were locked up in an asylum, they would leave me in a darkened room, and I would eventually just wither up and die, just like being in the dungeon. The truth for that eight-year-old child was, "If I ever become a famous author, I'm going to die." But not just die – I would die a painful dark death, suffocating, alone in the dark. I had lived with that poison buried inside my soul ever since.

Inside my apartment a few hours later, I had to lie down and suddenly started shaking violently as I had a feeling memory of the closet that was a dungeon. I felt suffocated, I smelled dust, I could feel shoes rub against my side, I was sure I was going to die that night. It felt like it lasted forever. I felt myself about to throw up, and had to fight a gag response, because my stomach hurt horribly. I didn't know where I could turn, who could get me out. No one was coming, and they would just forget about me, because that awful doctor ordered them to leave me there. I was trapped, smothered, and all alone. Then it was like I could visualize Doctor Crowder, looking through a narrow slot into my tiny asylum room, his malignant eyes crinkled up in a smile. I was so terrified I couldn't move. The slot closed, the lights went off, and I was alone in the dark.

Finally, the feelings subsided. I just lay there, numb and completely worn out. Then I remembered something that now felt really bizarre. One of Mamaw's favorite things was to buy me a milk shake when she drove me to my other grandmother's house. She would smile and giggle and tell me I was really special to her. She was like a little girl who needed my approval, wanting to make sure I "liked her best."

Part Five

Freedom's Just Another Word

Chapter 25: Insomnia – A Writer's Night Journey

F or the next several days after I did the inner child exercise, I lay on my bed with my arms and legs shaking for long periods of time. On one level I knew I had just freed a deep trauma from my soul, and the fears that had been stored in my body were breaking loose, but while it was going on – it was horrible. I would hold my breath, I was highly anxious, my heart thumped where I could feel it, and I was terribly sensitive to noises around me. Gradually each evening the feelings subsided, and I could sleep – sometimes not until dawn. Laying awake in complete fear most of the night was becoming my way of life.

In January 1988 I remembered a violent incident with my dad, and would lay awake until 3 a.m. regularly, unable to sleep and shaking with fear – the abuse happened very late at night, and it was unsafe to relax or sleep. I wasn't going to sleep well until the trauma worked its way through my body and released, so I took a night job for three years, and worked from 11 p.m. to 7 a.m., until I could once again sleep at night. That experience gave me trust in the process that if I could just hang on and let the feelings break free from what happened with Mamaw, it would have a powerful healing impact. But I intuitively sensed that the abuse was deep and powerful, and would take some time to work through.

Returning to work while the fear was releasing would be difficult. I was faced with the prospect of being awake and in distress late at night fairly frequently as the fears released, with no way to control it. Trying to work under those conditions would be terribly stressful – probably unsustainable. I mentioned to a friend that for the moment I was "virtually unemployable." It took a while for that to sink in. Because of the inability to work, my original plan to publish the book in January 2009 might be too far in the future. It might be time to take a gamble, and an option to publish the book resurfaced, again to be considered, only with a different time frame.

I could arrange things financially where I would not have to take another contract in the oil business for a while. By doing that I could let the fears purge without trying to maintain a work schedule. As long as I couldn't work anyway, I might as well go ahead and publish the book. I wrote that down as Plan B, and put it in an envelope, to be opened a month later, to see if it still sounded like a wise move. I set the envelope on a bookshelf in my apartment, and let it go for the moment. At the moment I was still feeling the effects of the grandmother incident, and didn't want to try to make a decision while the fears were releasing. I would discuss the new plan with my friends Karen, Gregg, and Scott, to see what they thought about it. I prayed for God to show me a sign if I should go in that direction.

The next day, I told Karen about it, and after going through the whole thought process, she said the plan sounded solid. Gregg and Scott agreed. I checked out the Print on Demand publishers, and reviewed the whole publishing model. One article indicated that a lot of big companies were in the business of selling services to authors, and weren't necessarily interested in helping an author actually sell books. The article mentioned a small publisher that appeared to be a preferable option.

This smaller company used the same distributor as the larger publishers, but didn't try to sell the additional services. I checked out their website, and it looked very credible. The publisher could typically put a book into publication within a month. They didn't accept all authors, because they were a small shop, but the author would get more personal attention. The larger Print on Demand publishers took four to five months to get published, and adding in my time to finish the book, that would have pushed publication into early 2009. I had a window of time to publish the book now, and with the smaller publisher, a way to make that happen.

About the same time, I got an email from Sandra, a friend I had gone to high school with in Farmington, New Mexico. We began to exchange emails, and it brought up a lot of memories and feelings. I had known Sandra and many of my friends in Farmington since grade school. When my family had abruptly moved in the middle of my junior year in high school it devastated me, and I had never gotten the chance to say goodbye or get any closure with the kids I had known.

In July, there was a forty-year reunion for the class of 1968, and Sandra asked if I was going to attend. Even though I didn't graduate in Farmington, since I still had a strong emotional connection to the school I decided to attend the reunion, to be able to visit with Sandra. She had a perspective on my early years that I wanted to hear about. She had always been an insightful person, and she would be able to illuminate what I had looked like to others back then. My trip in January had given me new insight on the power of Farmington, and why I was so strongly bonded to it. I had to go to the reunion. There was some connection between moving forward on publication, and revisiting the place of my youth.

Just doing research about Print on Demand publishers forced the fears to purge more intensely. I had to let the fears release – if I avoided them, they would continue to fester and poison my insides; my fear was that I would abandon another project to publish a book, like I had done twice before. That thought wasn't much comfort each night when I lay awake, my legs shaking with fear, feeling unsafe.

Chapter 26: A Writer Prepares to Publish

I t seems dumb to take actions that bring up fearful and terrified feelings. But that was what I had to do. By moving toward publication, I was taking steps to confront those fears and false beliefs instilled by Mamaw, get them to the surface, help me release them, and ultimately be free of them.

Since the early '80s when I had first gotten serious about writing, and set the goal to publish a book, 11 p.m. signaled the onset of the nightly terrors. I would exercise after work, be suitably tired and ready to go to sleep. I would lie down in bed, and suddenly my eyes would snap wide open, my body would go on high alert, I'd feel tremendously sensitive to noises, my breathing would become short and shallow, and my pulse would race. It was like that tonight. Footsteps on the stairwell outside my apartment, innocent in daytime, took on an ominous tone. *Who was it and were they dangerous? Were they coming to get me?* I felt like an eight-year-old child, listening to Mamaw tell me they could have me committed, locked up in an asylum for a couple of days, just to show me what it would be like.

Was this the night they would come get me? My rational adult mind knew that not to be the case, but the mind of the terrified child ruled the night. I listened until the footsteps faded, a door opened and closed, and the threat passed – for the moment. I still couldn't relax, and was wound up tightly; ready to bolt out the door or jump off my third-floor balcony into the bushes below if that was the only way to escape. My fears grew larger, more menacing. A bird trilled outside my apartment, and I was back inside the bedroom at Mamaw's house, windows wide open to the night, with the lights out, sensing the dangerous closet, fearing the monsters that might still be inside. My legs shook uncontrollably. I was powerless to stop anyone who might come to get me.

One night as I lay on the bed shaking, I remembered years ago turning on the TV to a scene from *One Flew Over The Cuckoo's Nest*. It was obviously the inside of an asylum, and I quickly changed the channel. I had never been able to watch that movie. Now the dismal hospital scene with patients in a daze trudging slowly around the ward inflamed my overly active imagination. My stomach got queasy and I felt my muscles tense – ready for escape. Finally the safety of daylight came, and I drifted off to sleep.

When I remembered the violent incident with my dad in 1988, I concluded the late-night high alert I went into was about the violence with him. The anxiety had always been worse on Saturday nights because some of the violence with my dad happened then. But now it made sense that the events with Mamaw were part of the sleep problems. Mamaw would take me over to the house of my other grandmother on Sunday, when she was still off work. So the closet incident with her may have happened on Saturday night. I started writing *Search For Peace* in 1985; about the same time the late-night inability to sleep had started. Snapping awake at 11 p.m. may have been very much about Mamaw.

While I battled through sleepless nights, awake until very late and releasing fear, I still moved toward publication. I had found a Print on Demand publisher which looked like a good fit for me, but they had indicated they preferred to have an author with a website. I began to set up a website. Immediately moving toward publication felt like the true direction for me. Exactly a month after I had written my Plan B, I made a little ceremony about taking the envelope down from the bookshelf and opening it. The direction still sounded solid, so I committed to go ahead and pursue publication of the book.

I signed up for the Agents and Editors Conference in Austin again, to check traditional publishing one more time before pursuing self-publication. When I went to that conference in 2007, the fears instilled by Mamaw began to bubble to the surface. I had what I thought was a stronger presentation to convince an agent to represent my book. The conference had open slots with literary agents, so I signed up for three total pitch sessions with agents. I had a stronger presentation and more meetings with literary agents – this was sure to force the fears to purge more quickly. I continued acupuncture every week, which helped release massive amounts of fear very quickly.

On May 27th, the website designer finished the final changes, and we went live with the website www.DanLHays.com. That morning I submitted my manuscript to the publisher I had chosen. The next day, that publisher passed on publishing the manuscript, without giving me a reason except that it wasn't suitable for them. They answered so quickly I concluded they hadn't even looked at the manuscript or my website. They gave me a suggestion for another publisher – Virtual Bookworm in College Station, Texas. This publisher actually felt like a stronger contact because they were only three hours from Fort Worth. I liked the idea of working with a company within driving distance if it was needed. I submitted the manuscript to them. The next several days the fear came up and purged a lot. During my Friday acupuncture session, I was actually shaking and releasing fear while I was on the table – the first time that had ever happened.

Virtual Bookworm replied in five days and accepted my manuscript for publication. I had one of their editors review the whole manuscript. I drafted a biography for the back cover, and went to a professional photographer and got pictures to use for the book cover, and in publicity efforts.

Now it was time to revisit the writer's conference that had started the healing process in motion.

Chapter 27: "I'd Like To Read Your Manuscript."

I t was June 2008, and I was in Austin at the Agents and Editors Conference for the second year, having a totally different experience than I did the previous summer. I had just walked out of what felt like a perfect pitch session with a literary agent. He had said those magic words, "I'd like to read your manuscript." I stepped into the foyer on the second floor of the hotel, turbulent with nervous writers waiting to pitch their manuscript, or walking into small rooms filled with literary agents sitting at cocktail tables, wanting to find that marketable manuscript. Things looked different than they had fifteen minutes ago. My life had just changed, and I ambled absent-mindedly to the elevator, stunned by what had just happened.

I got off the elevator in the hotel lobby and wandered around for a while, too keyed up to go into a workshop. I saw Terri, a writer I'd visited with the previous day. "Have you met with your agent yet?" she asked.

I smiled broadly. "I think I just had the perfect pitch session. It went wonderfully, and he asked to read a copy of my manuscript." I was amazed just hearing the words.

"Dan, that is excellent! Congratulations. Wow, you've had a wonderful weekend. Who was the agent?"

I told her the agent's name, and the agency he worked for. Terri's eyes got really big. "Dan, that is one of the most prestigious literary agencies in New York, and he is one of their most active agents. This is a big deal!"

I heard her words, but the news was so stupendous that I had trouble appreciating it. I could feel my eyes glaze over. Things had unfolded pretty fast.

The previous day I had checked in to the hotel, gotten settled, and went down to the conference rooms for a pre-conference workshop offered by a New York literary agent on "Pitching Your Manuscript." There were about fifty people in the room, and the agent started with a brief lecture on how to do verbal pitches. Then she said it would be more effective than a lecture if people were to actually try out a pitch. The agent wanted people to start with a very short pitch, and gauge the response.

"Who would like to try out their pitch in front of the group?" she asked.

Tentatively, someone raised their hand, got up, and delivered their pitch. More people followed, and it blossomed into an awesome session. I knew I had to do mine.

I raised my hand, and as I walked up, the agent said she knew me from somewhere. I told her I had been in the contracts workshop where she was a panelist last year. I gave my name, and then asked, "Have you got a minute?" She loved that and stopped me to give a brief lecture on respecting the space of the agents. I gave my brief pitch. "My book is entitled *Freedom's Just Another Word*. It's about a time when my life was spinning out of control, and then my dad died." She immediately began to tell the group about British "misery" literature – I hadn't portrayed my book correctly. She did respond strongly to the title, which people did a lot over the weekend.

After the workshop, I waited around and asked the agent if she had a moment, and we had a good laugh over that. "I'm just wondering how I can improve my pitch. I think I'm doing something wrong, because you compared it to British misery literature, and this book is definitely not that."

"What is your book about that is different from that type of work? What sets it apart?"

"Great question. I think it's the positive aspect – it's not about my dad dying as much as my healing journey from wounds that had kept us at a distance from each other. It's a very spiritual and uplifting book."

"That doesn't sound like the book you described to me in the pitch. I think you might want to lead with the positive perspective, and work from that place. Then agents will have a more accurate picture of your book."

"Excellent feedback. Thank you so much!"

I needed to completely rework my presentation of the book – what I had been doing so far hadn't worked. After dinner I went back to my hotel room to rethink things. Most of the evening was spent very thoughtfully revising the entire pitch. I started from the positive elements, and crafted, refined, and honed the wording. The new presentation felt strong and positive, and correctly reflected the manuscript. I spent the remainder of the evening walking back and forth in my hotel room practicing the presentation. It felt really solid. To adequately describe my book required a longer pitch, but it was worth the gamble that I could hold the attention of an agent.

The next morning I went up to the second-floor foyer for my first pitch session. The staff person said the literary agent was very friendly and just wanted a visit type session. I hadn't done much homework, and didn't know much about him, except that he had gone to The University of Texas School of Journalism in Austin. The lady led me in to a room with about six cocktail tables, occupied by agents in muted conversations with other writers.

I sat down, shook his hand, and asked, "So how is it being back in Texas?"

He smiled and said, "It's really nice being back down here. My dad is coming in from Corpus Christi, and I have a sister who lives in South Austin."

I smiled. "I bet that will be great. I also have a sister in South Austin. This is just a fun town to visit." He asked me what my book was about, and I began to describe it:

"I have written a memoir entitled Freedom's Just Another Word. *It is about a spiritual journey of healing, hope, and forgiveness. It is set in Houston, Texas, in 1987. At that time, my life was spinning out of control. It was as if some mysterious force was at work, skewing my world. I was trying to remember something, to put together pieces, fragments, from my past. I felt like the man in* The Bourne Identity, *trying to remember something from his past, but seeing only fragments. I was out of work, broke, frozen on going to look for a new job, almost suicidal, and mystified as to why it was all happening. Then I got the phone call – 'Come home, your father is dying.'*

I delivered the eulogy at my dad's funeral. He was an alcoholic, but he had been sober and in recovery for twenty years. A number of people told me the week he died how much he had positively impacted their life. He and I had also had a lot of healing over the past several years, so I spoke from a warm and loving place.

But over the next several weeks as I struggled with his passing, I started finding an ugly, deep anger toward him. It felt disloyal to be feeling that way. I uncovered an old wound that made everything begin to make sense, and to allow me to really forgive my father."

Dan L. Hays

As I talked, the agent was totally focused, concentrated on my words, and nodded several times. I stopped speaking and waited anxiously.

He got the title immediately, making a reference to the Janis Joplin song, and how much he loved it. Then he asked, "So what was the old wound?" I described the violent incident where my dad had threatened to kill me, and he was very intrigued. He was so intent on what I was saying, I had the feeling he had found something he'd been looking for, and was very interested.

"So what's your writing background?" he asked.

"I wrote a book in 1985 that a publisher from the West Coast was interested in, but I backed off. It was my recovery journey, and they were a recovery publisher. Then I wrote a novel in 1993 about my dad called *Nothing Left To Lose*, which will actually be the bookend for this current book, and I backed off from that one as well."

"What happened to that book?"

"I still plan to publish that novel, and probably rework the earlier book and publish it as well."

"Why do you think you backed off those earlier books?"

I smiled and said, "That's a good question. It turns out there were underlying issues – now being resolved – that kept me from publishing a book, which will be the subject of my next memoir."

He nodded, satisfied with that answer.

Our time was almost up, so I said, "Just to let you know, I'm moving forward with plans to self-publish this book by the end of the summer if nothing else works out."

He immediately pulled out a business card and handed it to me. "I'd like to read your manuscript before you self-publish. I'm a fast reader, and can have you an answer pretty quickly. But I would like to have the chance to read it."

"I'll send you a copy." I shook his hand, said goodbye, got up, and walked out of the room, to go reflect on the amazing pitch session. That was when I ran into Terri, and realized the power of my meeting was even greater than I had imagined.

A few hours later, I had the second meeting with a literary agent. He was very friendly, and appeared positively inclined toward my manuscript. It didn't fit for him, but he told me he liked what he heard, and wished me well. The third literary agent was very positive, but said the manuscript wasn't the sort of thing he represented. He referred me to a colleague in Chicago, and said to use his name when I queried her. By the positive interactions, I was on the right track about how to portray *Freedom's Just Another Word*.

Later in the weekend, I sought out the literary agent who had held the pitch workshop. "I just wanted to let you know I completely revised my pitch based on your suggestions." I told her about the positive responses I had gotten from my pitch meetings.

"I'm so glad to hear that," she replied. "That is an outstanding outcome – congratulations."

"Thank you. I just want to say thanks to you as well – you helped me shift the perspective on my book for the pitch, and it made all the difference."

"You are very welcome. Come back next year and tell me how it went!"

I suspected I might have some feelings to deal with – my manuscript was about to be read by a reputable literary agent — at his request. I was glad I had made plans to attend the high school reunion – it would keep me distracted and help minimize the anxiety while I waited to hear something.

Chapter 28: A Writer Revisits High School

I was back in Farmington, for the second time in six months. It felt odd to return so soon, but I always drew strength from being in that town, and attending the high school reunion promised to be revealing.

The first day I had lunch with Sandra at a restaurant downtown. It was great to catch up, but I also wanted to hear how others perceived me back in those days. I told her what my world at home looked like.

"My dad was drinking a lot when we were in junior high. I would come home from school, and never knew what to expect. If it had been a rough day at work, and he was in a bad mood, he would drink a lot, and things might get ugly. One of the incidents was over the Scholarly Scribbles magazine – I had published poems, and he got all bent out of shape about it, and yelled at me that I'd never amount to anything. That really hurt. Other times he was hitting me."

"Dan, I'm really shocked. I never would have guessed you had anything like that going on. You were always very poised and self-confident in school, especially Mrs. Kerr's class. You were probably the smartest one of our group."

"Sandra, that is so odd to hear. I never felt self-confident. I think I must have been good at covering up what I really felt."

"You must have been. I always thought you had a good chance to be the class valedictorian when we graduated. Everyone liked you – the jocks, the smart kids – you got along with everybody."

Her observations were a shock – seeing through someone else's eyes how I looked when I was a teenager was a revelation. Her impressions differed greatly from how insecure I felt back then.

The opening event of the reunion on Friday night was a happy-hour gathering at the VFW hall. I walked in feeling really awkward because I wasn't technically a graduate. I visited with a few folks, remembering some of them, and saw a lot of people I didn't recognize or barely knew. The group then moved over to the lounge at the Best Western motel to sing karaoke. I didn't feel like I really belonged with this group, and had started to wonder if this whole thing was a mistake.

Saturday evening I sat in my car outside San Juan Country Club. Inside, the dinner and dance for the Farmington High School reunion was about to start. I sat there, just looking at the building. This was something I never did in high school – go to a school dance. I had a snapshot memory of me and my friend Bobby, as we sat in his car outside the high school cafeteria, slumped down in our seats. We watched through the windows as the kids from our class smiled and danced after the football game. It looked like everyone was having a lot of fun. We didn't go in. Being small for my age and very shy, I had spent my high school years on the outside looking in.

In the middle of my junior year, my family moved away, and life was too turbulent to think about dances. I had never been to a reunion, because I didn't feel connected with the high school where I eventually graduated. Farmington was the town I grew up in, where I'd had a lot of friends, and lost touch with all of them after I moved. This reunion would be a chance to get closure.

I was going to the Saturday night event because it was paid for, and a couple of guys I had known since junior high had re-gathered their band and were playing for the dance. They had started the band after I moved away, and I'd never seen them play. Since I didn't really feel like I fit in, my plan was to have dinner, listen to the guys play a couple of music sets, and then leave. I checked my email once more from my cell phone, and answered a message about getting my book set up to be self-published. I was also waiting very anxiously to hear from the literary agent who was reading my manuscript, so I checked email often.

It was time to go inside, and my stomach was in knots at being in the big reunion event around people I didn't know very well. There was no more reason to stall, so I gathered my courage, got out of the car, and walked into the country club. The whole interior looked different – I guess a remodel after forty years was to be expected. I had spent a lot of time at the club growing up, learning to play golf, taking swimming lessons or playing in the pool, and occasionally having lunch with my dad. The country club had a lot of memories attached to it.

Not all the memories were that great. In seventh grade, a group of kids from our class took ballroom dance lessons at the Episcopal Church on Wednesday nights. We learned the fox trot, waltz, cha-cha, and the bossa nova, popular at the time. The class graduation was a dance out at the country club in the smaller ballroom. Most of the kids spent the evening out on the dance floor, but I was really small at that age, too shy to ask a girl to dance, and felt awkward and really embarrassed the whole evening. I didn't know how it would feel, coming back to this club, to once again sit and watch other people at a dance.

I walked into the main ballroom, where one side was filled with tables covered with white tablecloths, and set up with elegant china and silverware. In the middle of the room was a sizable dance floor, and a band was setting up against the far wall, in front of a bank of windows. I got a nametag – they had our high school picture on them, so we could recognize each other. I was on time, and being used to events where everyone was "fashionably late," was surprised at how crowded the room was, with a steady hum of chatter. People were already filling plates from the buffet. I spotted Elizabeth, who had lived next door to me in junior high, and walked over to visit with her and meet her husband. There was an empty place at their table, so I sat next to them for dinner. Elizabeth had brought several yearbooks, which we looked through as we visited. Yes, the homecoming queen our senior year was who I thought it would be – the girl I'd had a crush on since junior high.

We talked about Hermosa Junior High. Elizabeth had her copy of Scholarly Scribbles, the literary magazine we compiled in our eighth-grade English class. I was surprised to find that four different people still had their copy. I had published five poems and a short story in that magazine. Shortly after that, I had stopped writing altogether, later to find out it was because my dad had shamed my poetry, which shut down my creativity. I was impressed that the magazine had a strong impact on others as well.

While the band was testing equipment I walked out onto the dance floor to talk with Jimmy, the lead singer. I had a feeling that would be the only time I'd be on the dance floor that night. We talked about the popular girl who had disappeared – she had gotten pregnant, and we'd never known about it. He asked if I remembered each day during lunch having a competition to see who could walk the farthest on their hands. I smiled – I remembered it well.

Jimmy told me one of his memories. Our Civics teacher had called us a group of "pretentious pseudo-intellectuals." We laughed over that, because that's how we remembered that particular teacher – a pretentious pseudo-intellectual who was very self-impressed. I mentioned that Mrs. Kerr, our ninth-grade English teacher, had told Sandra years later that our class was one of the most vibrant, intelligent, and enjoyable groups she had ever taught. Junior high had been an almost magical time for me, and the Scholarly Scribbles literary magazine captured the essence of that time.

Kevin, the very popular star football player, came in with his wife, and quickly became the center of attention, causing quite a commotion by his entrance. Kevin might not recognize me now – I had been quite a bit smaller in junior high. He had lived down the block from me during grade school and we had known each other pretty well, so I'd go up later and re-introduce myself. I felt disconnected from much of the group – it appeared they had all stayed in touch and knew about each other's lives. I still felt like an outsider. When we were in school Farmington had been an oilfield town, so a lot of people came and went as their parents got transferred. When we moved I was quickly pulled out of school in the middle of my junior year and essentially disappeared. It was apparent that I would leave this dinner/dance soon.

Later that night, as I whirled around the dance floor to a country western tune, a woman I had liked in junior high snuggled in my arms, it struck me that the dance sure hadn't turned out like I expected.

Chapter 29: The Healing Dance

The reunion meal wound down, and the band was about to play, which was good – I could listen for a set and leave. During dinner Elizabeth and I had visited and reminisced, especially about our junior high days. Then Elizabeth and her husband got up to leave – they had to attend his reunion in Aztec. I was left at the table with two couples I didn't know, who were talking among themselves. Noticing an empty seat at a table next to the dance floor, I walked over and asked one of the women if I could sit there, to watch the band play. The woman was Lisa, who I had known in junior high. She introduced her friend Melanie, a tall blonde who didn't go to high school with us. She and Lisa worked with David, a local surgeon who was about to play guitar with the band. Melanie had come to support her friend and to see David play. She said she might want to dance some, but didn't like country western music. She'd tried it once or twice, and didn't find it fun. I tried to convince her it could be enjoyable, and she said she might give it a try.

While we listened to the band tune up, a woman walked up to me. She smiled and said, "Hi there. I'm at a table of women who are wondering who you are."

I was puzzled, but said, "I'm Dan Hays. I went to Ladera Elementary, Hermosa Junior High, and FHS – but my family moved away in the middle of my junior year."

She smiled, nodded, and said, "Good to know. I'm married, but that table of single women over there wanted to know who you were." Huh? I hadn't noticed anyone looking at me. Now I was intrigued.

The band started to play, and I convinced Melanie to try a slow two-step. We stepped out and began to ease around the dance floor. She was a great dancer, and said she really enjoyed herself. The band played a fast song, and we stayed out on the floor. I love fast dancing, and gyrated easily around the floor, wearing a big grin because I enjoyed it so much. I saw people watching me from the tables, and warmed at not feeling invisible. I had spotted the table of single women, and they moved out and began dancing around me and smiling at me. Later I went over and asked Jennifer to dance, an attractive brunette I had known in junior high. It was one of those amazing experiences where you escort the woman to the floor and transition from walking to dancing seamlessly. It was enchanting.

Finally I had to stop and rest for a minute – I was drinking glass after glass of water. Kevin, the football star, was walking by, and I introduced myself. He was amazed, and knew exactly who I was. Several of his buddies had talked with me at the VFW event on Friday night, and they were now watching me. There was a lot of attention focused on me, both because of the dancing, and because of talking with the class popular guy. I loved the whole experience.

Later, as the dance wound down and I slow-danced with Jennifer – I'd been alternating between dancing with her and Melanie for the past hour – I was once again astonished at how differently this reunion turned out than I had expected. Things felt really good right then. During the next fast dance, Kevin wanted to fist-bump with me out on the dance floor, which I did, and it felt good because of the acceptance it signaled.

The next morning I drove back to Texas, reflecting on the reunion. Something special had just happened – the dance had healed old pains from my youth. Being around people who knew me in childhood had also helped me reconnect with my innocence. I felt once again the vision of my future when I was six years old, where I knew clearly my destiny was to be a writer. It was very empowering to reclaim that vitality – I could use this newfound strength to attack the Mamaw messages.

I had two strong directions in place as a writer, either with the self-publishing company, or if the literary agent agreed to represent me. It was really exciting, but it brought up some of the Mamaw fear as well.

Once I got home, what I really wanted to do next – was pull out my copy of Scholarly Scribbles, and just read.

Chapter 30: Success

I couldn't wait to hear back from the literary agent who had expressed interest in my book, and kept checking my email often for word from him. After I went to the reunion in Farmington, I kept working toward self-publication. After three weeks, I hadn't heard back from the agent, so I sent a follow-up email. I was puzzled – he had said he could read it and get me an answer quickly, but this didn't feel very quick. Soon I would have to decide whether to wait on the agent, or move on. The book was scheduled to be self-published in early August.

Finally I got a reply from the literary agent:

"Many thanks for sending me your manuscript *Freedom's Just Another Word*. While there is much to admire here, I am not confident that it is something I could place with a publisher in today's highly competitive market. I hope you find someone who disagrees and wish you the very best of luck with it."

Honestly, looking back, I didn't let myself feel the disappointment of this rejection. The literary agent had reacted so positively when I described my book that his reply was a surprise. I thought he might at least suggest further work needed, and ask to see the book after that was done. I was glad that I had continued moving forward on self-publication, and we finalized that process. The excitement of what happened next covered up my disappointment. I got to say those magical words:

"I am a published author."

Just saying the words almost rendered me speechless. It was just too amazing, too incredible, to realize that I had just published a book. I went to the Amazon website on August 6th and found a listing for *Freedom's Just Another Word*, then just sat there and looked at the entry. I would get up, go do something else for a while, then come back and look at the listing. It hadn't changed, but I couldn't wrap my head around it.

The damaging messages by Mamaw had held me back from publishing two previous books. Her words "They'll call you crazy," "I can have you committed," and then when her showing me what it would be like to be in an asylum, had really locked up my writing. I had wondered if those old messages would intrude and keep me from publishing the current book, but it hadn't happened. When I actually saw the Amazon listing – there was visible proof that I had broken past, I had moved beyond. No wonder I was stunned and numb.

This was a line of demarcation – one of the three significant transition points of my life. The first was working the wheat harvest to walk in my dad's shoes – to find his story.

The second was completing my first marathon. The third – publishing this book. All three events had the flavor of a rite of passage, where I had crossed a threshold. I returned from harvest a changed and healed man in a very intense way. Crossing the finish line of my first marathon gave me a new sense of what I could accomplish. With publishing my first book – I had confronted and overcome old demons in a very tangible way.

I intuitively sensed that it was too soon to begin the next phase, so I made no immediate plans to line up any publicity. Later in the month, I sent inscribed and signed copies to several people to thank them for being part of the process. There was some emotional release, but I was still stunned at what had just happened, and I think that's why I didn't feel much fear. Also, I hadn't publicized the book or told many people about it. It was likely that getting the word out about my book would stir up some old feelings to be released.

I was a published author. I had succeeded.

Chapter 31: A Hopeful Omen

One night I had a dream:

I was asleep in the back bedroom at Mamaw's house. I woke up out of a deep sleep, and went over to the TV to try to fix the Nintendo so I could play a game. I turned and was surprised to see my dad. He had an amused smile on his face from seeing how startled I was by his presence. He left. Then my sister Kitty was there, helping clean out the house so they could sell it. I went into the kitchen to fix myself some soup. The stove was ancient and I couldn't figure out how to turn on the gas – I finally did. The refrigerator was already gone, and I was amazed at how small the kitchen was.

As I walked past the dining area, I could see places where the paint had chipped and exposed several layers of old paint underneath. The phone rang somewhere in the back of the house, and I went to the back bedroom to answer it. The furniture was all gone, and someone had just cleaned the carpet. It was very bright and cheerful in the room, with the back door and all the windows open, and a cool breeze blowing through. I didn't want to step on the just-cleaned carpet, and the room was empty anyway. I couldn't see a phone. I went to the cordless phone in the living room.

I saw a guitar and amp stacked to one side – I knew they belonged to a friend of Kitty's. I looked out the front door and the yard was paved – I knew they were going to turn this and several other houses into low-rent housing. I answered the phone, and it was some woman, calling about ... she hesitated, obviously trying to read from some notes, but getting confused. I told her if she figured out what she was calling me about to call me back, and I hung up.

The dream ended.

My dad had died in 1987, and my sister Kitty had died in January 2008, so when I had this dream inside Mamaw's house, with both those people present, it affected me deeply. I reconnected with a sense of family in some way. More than that, the tone of the dream had some pretty amazing aspects to it – signals about the healing process I was moving through. In the dream, I was amazed to have the strong sense that the back bedroom of the house where I had felt so isolated and unsafe had been purged of the negativity and was now clean and bright. Of course, I was also realistic enough to realize that dreams sometimes signaled where we wanted to be, not where we actually are, so I didn't take this dream to mean that I was completely healed. My gut said that wasn't the case, but I still very much liked the direction.

Chapter 32: Publicizing The Book

After a few weeks of sitting with the awareness that I had just published a book, I began to explore ways to publicize *Freedom's Just Another Word*. It would have been great to get TV exposure, but all my research indicated that an interview on television was hard to secure, and an author could spend a lot of money and time trying to grab that prize. On the other hand, it was fairly easy to get exposure through radio interviews, and not nearly as expensive as television. Plus, radio interviews didn't require travel – they could be handled while I sat at home. I investigated how to line up radio publicity.

In early September I signed up for ad space on Radio and TV Interview Report (RTIR) magazine, used extensively by radio stations. My research had indicated it was a great resource for securing radio interviews. I bought an ad for the issues that would be published November 1st, November 15th, and December 1st, and then worked with the copywriter to draft copy for the ad. He did an excellent job with it, and I was very pleased.

During September, I signed up to have my book listed on the Title Page with the Texas Writer's League. I put my name in for a lottery to win a two-hour slot to display my book at the Texas Book Festival in November at the Capitol in Austin. I continued to put it out there about the book I had just published.

The first request for a radio interview came from an unexpected source. Howard, a man I had known in Albuquerque, had always asked about my progress with the manuscript. I sent him an email to let him know that I had finished the book and it had been published. He replied an hour later saying he had moved to Palm Springs, California, and now co-hosted an Internet radio program called Journey to Wellness Now. He asked if I would be a guest on his program to talk about my book. It was unexpected, but I quickly agreed. We set up October 18th for the interview. Since I already knew Howard, I was comfortable with him, and the interview went well. We spent about thirty-five minutes discussing various aspects of the book.

After the interview with Howard, nothing much happened in terms of publicity. The radio magazine ads weren't out yet, and book sales continued to be slow. I had expected to get some feedback from people who had read the book, but things were conspicuously quiet. I remembered hearing Jack Canfield say that after his first book was published, it was initially met with a "thunderous silence." I could relate. I suspected the book could have a strong emotional impact on people, and might take a while for people to comment – but I wondered if I had totally misread my intuition that the book was about to build momentum.

I read my notes for my next memoir again, the Mamaw book, so my thoughts could continue to percolate about how to craft what I wanted to say. I still wasn't quite ready to write that book, or maybe Little Danny was just not quite ready to plunge into those painful events.

The first magazine ad came out on the first of November. I began to steel myself to not be disappointed if the publicity attempts with the ad yielded no responses.

The following Monday, things shifted dramatically.

The producer for a high-profile radio show contacted me. As I investigated, it became clear that the host was a powerful personality, and that this opportunity might open a lot of doors. We set up dates for December 18th and January 15th. She was excited to do the interviews, and sent me an email saying, "I got chills just from reading your book cover." I knew once she read the book, she would be really invested in the topic. This felt like a big opportunity. Her show was carried on World Talk Radio, boasting 5.5 million listeners, and archived on Ideocast. She also advertised my upcoming show on her website starting November 14th.

I got emails from a radio station in South Dakota and another in Longview, Washington, requesting interviews. The next day I had a voice mail to do an interview for a station in Lansing, Michigan. Things were picking up.

When I started conducting radio interviews to publicize the book, they followed a typical pattern. I would talk about the book in general, giving the title and a few thoughts from the introductory chapters. I would then allow time for the interviewer to ask questions or seek clarifications. We would move through the events of the book, leading up to the point where I remembered the violent incident with my dad, and how that explained so many things in my world. Over time I discovered the message was much the same, but I included more detail depending on the length of the interview.

One day I got a phone call from a station outside Rochester, New York. I had time for an interview right then, and the man had to run down the hall to the studio to record it. It was a great twenty-minute interview, and quite entertaining. I got the most off-the-wall question I've ever gotten in an interview. He asked, "Since you're from Texas, I've always wanted to ask about this. How do you feel the Dallas Police handled the Kennedy assassination?"

I was baffled at the question, and managed to say, "I was thirteen years old and living in New Mexico at the time. I don't really know much about that. Now about my book."

A few days later an email came in from an executive producer at VoiceAmerica (where the high-profile host broadcasted) to talk about me hosting an Internet radio show. I suspected this was a "Pay us and we'll teach you how to host" offer, but I wanted to see what she had in mind. It turned out my intuition was correct. The deal was for them to produce thirteen shows, and with them absorbing part of the production costs, I'd only have to pay around $13,000. The cost was humorously exorbitant, and I diplomatically declined. Hosting a radio show was something that had appeal, but it had to be the right situation.

I had coffee about that time with Cher, a woman I had known when I went to high school in Fort Worth. We had reconnected, and she had read my book. She made the most remarkable comment, saying, "Dan, your book has the power to take people to a universal place they might not know they have." This was a very insightful person, and a powerful statement, and gave me a deeper appreciation for the power of the book.

The second issue of the radio magazine ad came out November 15th, and the next day, I got an email from the producer for a late-night radio show to request an interview. The show was carried on two Internet networks and thirty stations around the country, so this would be excellent exposure for the book. The interview went very well, though the host wandered off topic several times, and pontificated about feelings – Karen thought he was upstaged by my presence and trying to not be shown up.

The next morning, I called Karen, and after we had talked for a few minutes she said, "What's going on with you?"

"What do you mean?"

"I mean your voice is high, and there's sort of a 'little boy' energy about you."

"I don't know. I wasn't aware of anything like that."

"You know what I think it is – you just opened up the door on the whole publicity thing with these interviews. You're really putting it out there. I think it's Little Danny – he's wondering if something bad is about to happen – like the guys in the white coats are about to show up."

I sat with that for a moment. "You know, that makes sense. I can sort of feel it now – like a low-level anxiety, almost below the surface."

"That's it. I think you'll get used to it soon – you just need to allow Little Danny time to catch up. I think he's still just in a watchful mode – he wants to see what happens."

"I bet you're right – it fits."

The host of the late-night show called Saturday afternoon to ask if I would be interested in doing media training. I knew he offered that service, and had expected some kind of pitch from him, but for him to call was pretty impressive.

He said, "I really connected with the anger thread in our interview, and know it would be a tough topic to present clearly. You don't need any training at how to do an interview, you did that part well (which was really great to hear), but I believe I can help you with how to best present your book. I will conduct a two-hour intensive session over the phone, write up most of the text for you to use, and work with you to polish it after you learn it."

The offer felt right and very solid, so I accepted. I did the training the next afternoon, and it was an incredible experience. He pulled out the essential elements of the book to present, and the best way to present them. He would write up text as I waited on the phone. The content he crafted was phenomenal, and well worth the money.

I worked on my radio presentation using the new techniques I had just learned, getting comfortable with the flow of how to let the topic unfold. During that time I was watching a lot of high school football, and would practice the presentation while driving to and from games. As well, the third magazine ad was published on December 1st.

On December 18th I did the interview with the high-profile radio show. It was disappointing. The woman who was hosting was really chatty, and seemed to want to show people how well she had read the book. I wasn't given room to elaborate and explain the book, and barely got a chance to slide in a couple of the points from the media training I'd just had. The woman dominated the whole conversation, and we talked about points in the book that a listener would only be able to understand if they had already read the book. It became clear that I needed to work on how to guide an interview.

The Amazon sales rankings for the book continued to drop over the holidays, and my website got very few hits. It didn't look like interest in the book was building from the radio interviews, especially the recent ones. No interviews came from the radio magazine ad that came out December 1st.

By the end of the month I was disappointed that the book had not picked up any momentum. I had apparently misread the signs that there was a spiritual hunger for this book, based on the feedback I'd gotten during my trip to New Mexico. Now it looked like I had slipped into magical thinking, getting into fantasy about what might happen.

I still felt effects as the Mamaw fears released – it was a lot of trouble to fall asleep. I was wide awake until 3 a.m. almost every night, feeling the fear, with my legs shaking. There was also a struggle with really old feelings – that God had deceived me. I had taken a path that was my best effort to follow God, things had gone astray, and I was not sure how I had veered off course. I also felt very vulnerable, as some of my friends weren't around. Karen had been unavailable recently, gone visiting her mom in Colorado. My longtime friend Gregg and I were scheduled to meet in early January, but that was the night of a college football bowl game, so we postponed. He said he couldn't see any times coming up in the foreseeable future to meet. With friends pulling away, I felt particularly exposed, at a time when I was taking risks and really needed the support.

Under the disappointment I could feel some anger – anger that things hadn't worked out with the book direction, and anger that longtime friends were not available. I wasn't sure what to do next.

Chapter 33: Minute To Freedom

One morning I did a ten-minute radio interview, for an 8 a.m. drive-time show. I wasn't sure how well my heavy topic would fit with a morning talk show. It was with a host named Kevin in Longview, Washington. It was a solid interview – he had either read the book or at least scanned the topic. He asked very insightful questions, and we had a great talk.

I had sent Kevin several signed copies of *Freedom's Just Another Word* as giveaways, and a couple of days after the interview, he emailed and asked if he could have a few more signed books – every time he mentioned giving a copy away on the air, the phone lines went crazy. I gladly sent him more books.

Several days later, Kevin suggested the possibility of doing one-minute features. When he described the concept, I didn't understand what he was talking about. It sounded like I would write one-minute-long talks on a specific topic. Then I'd get a voice professional to record the segments, and buy studio time to have them recorded. When I called a couple of recording studios, the costs to have someone record my text and professionally produce it were prohibitive.

I needed some clarity, so I called Kevin to ask about it. I told him that having the radio spots professionally produced was more expensive than I could afford.

Kevin told me he had something different in mind. He pictured short "golden nugget" segments, sharing an insight about my healing journey and recovery. That made a lot of sense – I had a lot of things I could talk about. I already could see topics in my mind, and they could flow pretty easily.

He then said for the audio, I had a great radio voice. He suggested that I record the segments myself – which would make them sound a lot more personal. Now I was getting intrigued. I had never recorded something like that, but suspected I could do it. He would record an opening and a closing, blend it with the audio I had generated, then use the studio to bring the whole segment up to professional standards.

It was a whole different concept than I had visualized, but it made a lot more sense. Kevin said my book had affected him deeply, would help a lot of people, and he wanted to be part of that. He would play the minute spots on his radio station, and see if their sister stations would be interested.

I did some research and realized that the parent company for his radio station also owned forty other stations along the West Coast. If we could get airtime on those stations as well as Kevin's, that could turn into a really exciting possibility. Recording the segments in my own voice had a whole different feel to it – it felt right. He suggested we call the series Minute to Freedom, which I really liked, because it captured the hopeful theme of the messages. The name also resonated with the title of the memoir, *Freedom's Just Another Word.*

I wrote the text for the first twenty radio spots, and felt well-prepared about how to present them, based on the media training I'd just completed. The content flowed very smoothly. I bought a high-quality microphone, and practiced recording the spots. On November 30th I sent Kevin a test audio. He loved it and said we were ready for production. I recorded the first twenty episodes and sent them off to Kevin. The result was amazing.

Kevin started airing the radio spots on December 8th. My voice was now being heard on the air daily, and it pushed old fears to the surface. I was doing my part to become a successful writer and spread the word about my writing and what I had to share. I kept shaking and releasing a lot of fear.

Episode topics kept coming very easily, and I sent audios to Kevin twenty at a time. Very quickly we had an inventory of one hundred *Minute to Freedom* topics. Kevin had said it would be most convenient if he hosted them on his website. That was great for me, because being connected with someone in the radio industry gave the audios tremendous legitimacy.

Then Kevin began to talk with publicity houses about developing a mailout to promote *Minute to Freedom*. A woman he knew at a publicity house offered to send out a blast email to approximately thirty-five thousand radio contacts. Because she knew Kevin, she would charge him a very inexpensive price.

At the end of January, the publicity company sent the email blast, which made me pretty nervous. The only response the next day was from Hillsboro, Texas. Then a station in San Luis Obispo said they might be interested. A couple of days later, a program director who managed two Clear Channel radio stations in San Francisco said he wanted to use *Minute to Freedom*. Both radio stations were talk-radio format, and one carried Lou Dobbs, Dennis Miller, and the big-time talk-show guys. Kevin and I agreed that the media blast had paid for itself right then.

Kevin said he got almost six hundred hits on his website where people downloaded one or more segments, so there were a lot more stations which might be thinking about airing the feature. I was pretty excited.

We now had four affiliates for *Minute to Freedom* – two of them Clear Channel talk news stations out of San Francisco. Things were looking really positive.

Chapter 34: The Publicity Effort Continues

I wanted to continue with the publicity efforts, but had decided not to do any more ads in *Radio and TV Interview Report* magazine – the results hadn't been all that great, and it was time to try something different.

The next day, a woman called from an interview booking service. It felt like a solid connection from the very beginning – it was like talking with Kevin, who had helped me with *Minute to Freedom*. She was reading my website as we talked, and said I was setting it up as if I were going to have a bestseller. She confided her father was an alcoholic, and that's why she connected with my material.

She then said, "You know, I just have to say this. I haven't booked for TV for a while, but people have been asking me when am I going to get back into it. I just have this feeling that you are going to be the one that gets me back into booking for TV." We started talking about shows like *Oprah*, where an appearance would be an amazing success for a writer, and how I would be open to something like that if it happened. She wanted me to do some radio interviews first, and talk with her media strategist, but she could definitely see TV being a possibility for me. (When I looked back on this later, I realized this person was really skilled at throwing out bait that would be of great interest to an author. It made me angry to go back and read this. I fell for it. She never pursued the TV option.)

She called again the next day, and was totally amazed after having read my entire website. I decided to go with her service, and agreed to start with a ten-interview package. I called Kevin in Longview and talked it over with him – he was on board and excited for me. He later told me he had some reservations, but I was so excited he didn't want to spoil that.

Next came a phone meeting with the company's media strategist that completely changed the dynamic of my interviewing. As I was telling her about myself, I made the comment that "In the '80s I was walking around Houston with PTSD and didn't know it."

She said, "Dan, let's stop right there for a minute. Post-Traumatic Stress Disorder is a really important topic right now – it's very much in the public awareness. I think that's the way to introduce your book."

I replied, "Honestly, I have a reservation about doing that. I don't want to come off sounding like some healthcare professional who has clinical expertise, because I don't."

"That's a great point. Why not preface your comments with, 'According to the American Psychiatric Association, the definition of PTSD is,' and then give the definition. Follow that with 'The symptoms are,' and then describe the symptoms as you experience them. That way you're not the expert; you're just quoting the experts. Then you can describe how those symptoms impact your life."

I thought about it for a moment. "I like that – I like it a lot. That's a solid approach, which doesn't make me sound like somebody I'm not. I'm just a guy with PTSD who describes my world, and talks about my healing process."

"Exactly, Dan." I smiled, because we had the missing piece to make my topic attractive to interviewers, presented in a way that was comfortable for me.

I had been aware since the 1980s that I exhibited PTSD symptoms, but I finally got solid confirmation in 2010. I had an evaluation done by a psychologist, who diagnosed me with Post-Traumatic Stress Disorder that was both "severe and chronic." He identified the source of the PTSD as twofold – the violence with my dad when I was seventeen, and the abuse by Mamaw when I was eight years old. It was shocking to see how elevated my symptoms were. He ran tests on ten scales to evaluate the level of trauma, and if three of those scales were elevated, it indicated clinical significance. My results were elevated on eight of the ten scales, and three of those scales were extraordinarily high. No wonder it had taken so much work, and been such a long, laborious process, trying to heal the effects of the violence with Dad, and the Mamaw abuses.

The media strategist then said, "It would be great if you could offer resources for people, like suggesting therapy, twelve-step or something like that – solutions when people searched Google late at night. That's something to think about – maybe you could put them on your website."

A few minutes later I asked her "How can we blend in *Minute to Freedom*? I'd like to use that resource in some way."

She looked at the segment list and said, "Those are the resources I was talking about – this is perfect!" Everything was coming together.

I then did five radio interviews, which helped me refine the message and how to present it. The down side was I saw no real bump in the Amazon sales figures, or the visits to the website.

———

Sunday, April 5th, I engaged in another kind of publicity. I talked to the Downtown Singles Sunday School Class at First Methodist Church, to share about my book. I did a lot of public speaking back in the '80s, and it was tremendously stressful. I would be in a lot of fear before I had to speak. For several days before this talk, I watched to see if the old issues about speaking in public would happen. Nothing came up – only mild pre-game jitters, which I considered a huge success. The talk was a powerful experience. I felt at home, comfortable, and felt very present as I shared about my book.

There were about forty singles in their sixties and seventies in the room, and I wasn't sure how well they would connect with my topic. After my talk they flooded me with questions, and many of them had been exposed to PTSD in one way or another. That experience with public speaking signaled I was ready to be visible and successful, and use speaking to complement my writing. I was seeing the fruits of the recovery work I had done.

Over the next week, it became clear that the interview booking service wasn't going to come through like I had hoped. The next interview they lined up was with a station where I had spoken six months ago, in a very tiny market in rural North Dakota. Looking at the client list for the service, I could see that there were a lot of common interview locations among the authors they represented. It appeared the booking service had a set of regular stations where they secured interviews, and most weren't very big markets. I wished I had checked that out sooner.

I wasn't going to use this booking company any more, but needed to have something positive to look toward, so I contacted another publicist and talked to her the next day. She said she could guarantee radio interviews in top-thirty-five radio markets. I began to research this publicist, and it felt like a good fit, but I'd thought that before, so I hesitated.

I thought about the whole idea of doing more publicity. Was it time to gamble on another publicist? Where was this whole publicity effort going? Was it time to just cut my losses? More to the point – was I trying to give up because the old Mamaw messages were still causing me to stop short? I had lots of questions at that point, but no firm answers.

Part Six

Moving To The Light

Chapter 35: Therapeutic Release

T alking with the media specialist about PTSD reinforced that the events with Mamaw were deeply buried, and the effects on my life were really strong. It was time to get some help with those issues, and do some therapy sessions to help break that energy loose. I'd heard good things about Eye Movement Desensitization and Reprocessing (EMDR), which was specifically used in abuse situations to help disconnect the memories from the abuse. I found a therapist named Jeannie who did EMDR, but who also used a newer type of related process called brain spotting, which accomplished the same thing. She felt this newer technique would be even more effective in my situation. I had a strong sense (or was it a wish?) that I was almost through with the Mamaw issues, but I thought this therapy would let me see where I was with my healing journey.

The concept of the therapy sounded kind of odd, but was highly recommended, so I was at Jeannie's office to give it a try. As the session began she said, "What we will do is identify a specific focal point about the incident – something that will bring up a mental image of that abuse for you. I will use this little pointer with the red button on the end of it, and have you follow it with your eyes, keeping in mind the focal point. I will move the pointer all around until I identify a specific spot. That is where the abuse incident is connected to your brain, through your eyes."

"What do I have to do?"

"You just sit there, keeping your eyes on the pointer. I will ask you to put on the headphones, and I will begin to make statements that counter the abuse. You'll be able to hear my voice, because the sounds will be really low – with soft music in the background. We will hold that eye focus for as long as we need to. I'll be able to tell when the abuse disconnects."

"How long will we have to do this therapy to have the incidents break loose?"

"It will depend on how strongly the abuse incident is still locked into your system. But it usually doesn't take more than two or three sessions."

———

In the first session we discussed the issues I wanted to work on. I thought it best to start by checking on the violence with Dad. I described what had happened – I came home late at night, found my dad sitting in the den with a high-powered rifle, and an abusive and violent incident followed. The focal point we selected was the gun he had held during the abuse. I put on the headphones, followed the pointer with my eyes until she stopped at a place a little above my eyes and to the right. She didn't do it long, and said, "There just wasn't much there. You must have done a lot of work, because it fell away pretty quickly."

"Yes, I've worked for a long time about that incident with my dad." I was astonished by how loose I felt – it felt like a door had shut or something. I grew more confident with the therapy.

The other and more vital issue was of course Mamaw. I described the things Mamaw had said – about being locked up, her doctor saying he could commit me to an asylum, her putting me in the closet to show me what it would be like.

"What do you think would be the focal point with Mamaw?"

I thought for a minute, and said, "Her evil grin. I can still see that grin vividly."

"Excellent. That's a great visual, and if it's that strong, it will register well."

I put on the headphones again. She began moving the pointer around, finally settled on a spot where I could feel my eyes twitch. She held on that point and she began quietly talking. "Visualize a world without that abuse. Imagine walking out of that closet, being surrounded by a bright, golden light, and your grandmother had never said those things. Get that mental image strongly in your mind." She then grew quiet, and just focused on the spot. After a time, she stopped.

"We have released the old limitations on those old memories."

I was astounded at how simple it had been. Later I realized the therapy method didn't work for me as the complete shortcut to healing which had been indicated. I'm not sure if the therapist overpromised or under-delivered, but the therapy didn't eliminate the issue.

"If you want to do a follow-up session, I'm available, but I believe you might not need it."

Later that week, I felt some old and deep feelings rise to the surface and release. They were all about God, and feeling despair, like when I was seventeen after the incident with Dad. It didn't last long, and I felt much more free with the Dad issues. A couple of days after that, I had a delayed reaction, and in a short time a huge amount of fear released, my legs shaking intensely. I did feel much lighter.

While adult Dan felt free, I sensed that Little Danny wasn't so sure. His feeling was still about being trapped, suffocating, about to die, and there was nothing he could do about it. I asked the therapist for another session, and she agreed. We did a second session, a very long one, where she had me visualize Little Danny leaving the closet and feeling safe. We released those messages, and I felt a wonderful sense of empowerment. For about three weeks after that, old fears released and just kept flowing out of my body for long periods of time. My legs shook violently almost every night. It was clear the therapy had accelerated the release of abuse feelings, so that part was really beneficial.

It still felt like something still hadn't quite released. We did a third session to deal with Mamaw, because fear of the woman was still coming up. That too released quickly. I was almost in shock as I realized the blocks were not there anymore, and I had set up the foundation to become very successful. I listened to a pre-recorded teleconference by Jack Canfield. Hearing what he had done to prepare himself as an author, I realized I was doing everything he had to be successful – even using visualizations and affirmations, which I had done for many years. It was a powerful awareness, and it continued to force the old Mamaw feelings to the surface. The next several weeks were really intense with releasing fear, but each time my legs and arms shook, and feelings released, I felt a little lighter.

We did a fourth and final session on March 14th. Little Danny didn't believe that we were free, and he was standing in the door of the closet, afraid to come out. She focused the whole session on Little Danny, and held the thought of releasing the old messages for a long time – about twenty minutes. The therapist was confident we had fully cleared out and disconnected the effects of what had happened with Mamaw.

Chapter 36: The Wounded Child

In early May I sensed that Little Danny was standing at the edge of the closet, unwilling to completely step out. He was afraid someone was still out to get him, and I could feel a knot deep in my stomach. For several days I had a feeling of impending doom – something bad was about to happen, and I was powerless to overcome it. I felt suffocated, panicky, weak, and helpless, totally helpless.

I woke up on Saturday morning, May 9th, reliving the old messages from Mamaw that had crippled Little Danny. It was a very vivid-feeling experience, as I felt what I was too numb to feel at the time the abuse happened. I couldn't breathe, it felt like it would have been better if I had never been born, and part of me was dying. I felt a deep anguish, felt hopeless, and helpless to do anything about it.

My dream to be a writer had died when Mamaw told Little Danny the bad things and made him step inside the closet, and I felt that loss all over again. I lay on my bed in complete agony and cried out to God. My voice was very high, like a little boy sitting curled up in a ball. "I am powerless over these old messages, and they are making my life unmanageable. I'm not sure that even

You can overcome them." I felt like Little Danny, sitting in the closet at Mamaw's house, unable to escape, about to die. I could smell the mustiness of the closet, and could feel the shoes against my hip.

Later that Saturday I got up and nothing happened for the rest of the day. On some deep level I knew I was trying to release the old Mamaw messages, but I couldn't do any more to overcome them. I felt a quiet sense of resignation that something had to happen, and I wasn't sure what that would be. Danny had lived with those fears for fifty years, and they were still choking the life out of his soul. It was his job to keep those fears from being realized – by holding me back from success as a writer. I prayed and surrendered it to God.

The fearful feelings were now coming up and releasing in the mornings – feelings I would have had after being shut up in the closet the night before. When I went to bed Saturday night, I suspected that Sunday morning I would go through another level of reliving the incident. I felt peaceful in a sense – if this was what it took to release those old feelings, I was ready. I was not happy about it, but I was willing.

I awoke Sunday morning aware that something had shifted, and I was in a different place. Little Danny was standing outside the closet surrounded by a golden light, and that knot of pain in my stomach was no longer there. My stomach hurt a little bit, almost like after surgery. I felt a marvelous warm sensation, a very peaceful feeling. It is my belief that God removed the abuse from my soul. I knew I couldn't have done it.

I prayed and communed with God more freely than I had in years. I was reconnected with God in a way that had been blocked since I was eight years old, when the bad things happened with Mamaw. The purpose of getting back the memories, releasing the old feelings, and doing the therapy work, had been to dig down to that deep well of feelings and release those old messages. I had to get right down to the bottom, to a place where I was powerless to do any more, to see that through my own efforts, I was powerless to release the effects of that old abuse and damage.

I began to reflect once more on that sense of destiny I'd had when I was young. The resurgence of energy that I first experienced after we released the messages in the therapist's office began to return. Little Danny had been afraid to boldly act upon that expectancy, when he still believed someone was coming to get him and something bad was about to happen.

My goal for the next week was to rest and let the whole experience sink in, since I was depleted and tired, and needed to be gentle with myself. It was like I had just gotten off an operating table after a most intense spiritual surgery. I walked around just trying to absorb this new place. I felt loved, and prepared by God in a very special way. I felt blessed and very humbled. I wanted to share the hope I had gained with others who had gone through similar abuse. I wanted to write about it, to share how powerfully the healing process had worked for me.

Chapter 37: Preparing To Leave The Scary Closet

T he next Saturday morning, a running group I belonged to went on a nine-mile training run. While I was out on the trail, I claimed victory in a very powerful way. It was a very profound and spiritual moment. It happened about halfway through the run. We were out on the Trinity Trail, and because I was slower, I had separated from the group. I whispered a prayer, an acknowledgement of the spiritual transition that had just happened, and was enveloped with a sense of peace all at once as I ran. I felt empowered to take the next steps, whatever those might be.

Moving to a new place once again forced old feelings to the surface, just as it had done many times. That evening the old doubts surfaced yet again for Little Danny – would God really be there for him? It felt like God had abandoned the little boy at age eight when the bad things happened. I asked God for a sign that things really had changed, and that it was not just my flighty dreams.

I began to shake, and released Little Danny's fears at a level I had never experienced before. I sat inside the darkened closet, feeling all the sensations of it. I felt choked by the musty closet, scratched by the rough wood against my back, sore from the hardwood floor I sat on. I heard the TV in the other room, occasional laughter from Mamaw. I felt a cramp in my stomach. I wanted to cry out, a primal scream of my terror, my abandonment. I couldn't, because it would only draw her back to torment me more. I whimpered in anguish. It was so hot that I felt suffocated. I didn't want to move because there might be spiders and snakes, and to move would make me touch them. Eventually the feelings subsided, leaving me drained and depleted.

That night I watched the movie The Horse Whisperer, and realized that Little Danny was like that terribly wounded horse, who needed gentle firmness to let go of the old abuse and way of life, to move to a new place of healing. The adult part of me would have to guide him out of that dark and scary closet and into the light, where he could live without that old weight.

I woke up Wednesday shaking, and cried out, "I can't leave the closet." Little Danny was still in fear that if he left the closet, the bad thing would happen – that asylum thing. I talked to Little Danny, letting him know that we would be gentle, but that it was time for him to leave the closet, and I wanted him to get ready. If the effort was too much for him, God would show a way to let him leave and feel comfortable, so that he would not try to go back.

I called my friend Carl, who I had known for many years from recovery circles. He was horrified when he heard what Mamaw did. His reaction helped me see more clearly how deeply she had poisoned my soul. I thought of my poem "Outside the Walls," written in 1986, which captured what was going on right now. It was about being free, but unwilling or unable to accept that freedom. At that moment, I understood the poem more fully.

Outside the Walls

I lived in prison for many a year,
Inside the four walls that I built with my fear.
The air was rancid, surroundings were stark,
I sat in my chains, alone in the dark.

The safety of prison, inside my cell,
No one could touch me, in my private hell.
I sat and pondered, what could be wrong?
I would not leave, so I sang my fear song.

God showed me a picture, life sunny and free,
I shrank in the corner, not wanting to see.
He drew me so gently, through the cell door,
Freed me to love, not keeping score.

Looked back at my prison, from down the road,
How massive the walls, my fear to hold.
They fell as I watched, rubble and dust,
I scarce could believe, but do so I must.

I felt very naked, the walls were not there,
People could see me, people could care.

I tottered along, mid flowers and grass,
With a foreboding that this too would pass.

My eyes grew stronger, facing the light.
I no longer hungered to hide in the night.
My step grew steady, bolder, more sure.
Freely accepting the loving so pure.

Friday, I woke up and began to pray. I just had a sense I wanted to do something that could affect me at a very visceral level. I remembered the scene in the movie Forrest Gump where Forrest bulldozed the house that had caused Jenny so much pain. I realized I could do an inner child exercise visualizing something similar. I would vividly picture tearing down Mamaw's house, so Little Danny could stand in the light without being afraid. It was time to let go of those harmful messages in a very visual way, a way that a child could understand. Then I could claim my destiny as a writer, and not avoid it any longer.

I just lay in bed reflecting on that thought for a long time. I could feel myself becoming prepared. I would perform some kind of ritual, and though I couldn't tell what it would be, I knew I would see the right way when it was time.

I was very aware that Saturday was July 4th – Independence Day!

Chapter 38: Independence Day

J uly 4, 2009. Independence Day. The inner child exercise had come into focus, and I knew how it would unfold. I wanted to show Little Danny Fear Child he really was free – able to leave behind the dark closet and all the messages from that abuse. I would visualize bulldozing Mamaw's house for Little Danny in clear and vivid detail, and for support, draw on a resource that would resonate for a child. I began to write:

"Danny?"

"Yes?"

"Are you ready to talk?"

"Yeah, I guess so."

"Great. You've been doing very well! You really have. These are tough old messages we've been trying to overcome. Do you get that?"

"Sort of – it's really scary. Mamaw was so sure about it all."

"Yes, Danny, I understand. But here's something I have come to understand recently – Mamaw was crazy. Just flat out crazy."

"She was? But she was a nurse, and I thought she knew a bunch of stuff."

"Who told you that?"

"She did."

"Exactly. I think she believed it in her mind, but it wasn't true. She was just a sick, twisted old woman who tried to hurt you really badly."

He thought a moment, and then nodded.

"Danny, here's another thing. She was really evil. Her sickness had turned in on her until she had a really nasty, evil side to her. Remember when the therapist asked what to use for the focal point of the incidents with Mamaw, and I said, 'Her evil grin.' She really did get pleasure out of causing you pain. That's very unfortunate. But Danny, I want you to really hear me on this. You did nothing wrong. Why don't you say it."

"I did nothing wrong."

"You didn't deserve to be punished."

"I didn't deserve to be punished."

"Mamaw was just a sick old woman."

"Mamaw was just a sick old woman."

"The things she said were not true."

"The things she said were not true."

"You can leave her behind now."

"I can leave her behind now." He paused, took a deep breath.

"How are you feeling?"

"My stomach feels funny."

"Maybe you're a bit scared?"

"Yeah, some."

"Danny, that is perfectly natural. You've lived with these deep, ugly messages, and the feeling of being put in that closet, buried in your soul for a long time. It's going to be a bit scary leaving that all behind. But why are we doing this?"

"So I can be happy."

"Exactly. And be free to do what?"

"To write."

"Yes, to write, but without living in fear of bad things happening. God wants you to be free to write. You have a lot to say, don't you?"

"Boy, do I!"

"So, Danny, just keep remembering that the reason we're doing this is to bring you joy."

He nodded.

"Remember when the therapist had you visualize stepping outside of the closet in Mamaw's back bedroom? The one she shut you up in that night?"

"Uh huh."

"What did it feel like?"

"It was like I was in a warm place, with a lot of light, and it was really safe."

"And there was nothing bad around you, was there?"

"No. I knew it was going to be okay."

"But it was hard to stay in that good place, wasn't it?"

"Yeah. I'm sorry, I just couldn't hold on to that good place."

"Danny, you don't have to apologize. You lived for fifty years with those old messages running your life. It takes a while to let them go."

He nodded again.

"Remember when we had that healing experience in May – when God healed what we could not, and removed the weeds of those old Mamaw messages from our heart?"

"That was pretty amazing."

"Danny, you were free at that moment – do you see that?"

"Yeah, I get that."

"But it was still hard to leave, wasn't it?"

"Uh huh. What if I did something that would make the bad things happen? I was scared to try."

"Yes, that's perfectly understandable. I can see how it would be hard to accept what had just happened. But remember last week when we were releasing some of the old fears? We were just clearing out the old messages in the corners of our soul, and there wasn't a lot of steam left in the old Mamaw messages. Remember what you cried out?"

"I said 'I can't leave. I can't leave the closet. It's too much.'"

"Yes, Danny. It's understandable you would have that fear, because those old messages were so deep. Remember that I told you then to start getting ready to leave. I wouldn't force you to go before you were ready, but it was time to leave Mamaw behind. Remember that?"

"Yes."

"How are you feeling about that now? Kind of nervous?"

"Yes."

"But are you ready?"

"Yes, I am. I'm tired of Mamaw."

"Danny, that's great. I'm going to show you in a whole different way that you are free of Mamaw, and can leave those messages behind forever. Are you ready?"

"I sure am."

"Excellent. Danny, do you remember the movie Forrest Gump?"

"Oh yeah, I liked that movie a lot!"

"Remember when Forrest had a bulldozer knock down the house that had caused Jenny so much pain?"

"Sure."

"Well, we're going to do that to Mamaw's house today."

He got very thoughtful.

"What are you feeling?"

"That feels – I don't know how to say how it feels. Good. Neat. So her house, the closet, all of it, will be gone? I like that."

"Good. First, imagine yourself back in her house." He nodded. "You are standing in the closet in her back bedroom." Little Danny gave a small shudder. "As you look out of the closet, there's a bright golden light like we pictured in the therapist's office. So there are no scary things in there. What does that feel like?"

"It's really nice."

"Good. Danny, do you remember Aslan the lion in The Chronicles of Narnia?"

"Yes, I liked him a lot."

"What did he represent?"

"God. Jesus."

"He was pretty powerful, and golden, wasn't he?"

"Oh yes, he was enormous, and you knew he wasn't a tame lion, but you felt safe with him."

"Yes, I agree, Danny. I want you to picture the lion standing in the middle of that back bedroom. Take your time. See him?"

"Oh yes – that is amazing."

"Danny, here's what we're going to do. When you're ready, you're going to take my hand, and we're going to step out of the closet, and go to the lion."

He nodded, and then thought about that for a long time. The lion stood there placidly, watching us, in complete repose.

Finally I said, "Danny, are you ready?"

"Yes."

"Good. Then take my hand." He did, and then we stepped forward. We took two steps and were past the door of the closet. I heard his breath catch, but he kept walking, until we were standing in the middle of the back bedroom, next to the lion.

"Danny, you can pet him if you want. He'll let you." He stroked the lion's fur very gently for a long time. Finally he stopped and looked up at me.

"Danny, I want you to hold on to the lion, and then we're going to walk out of the house." He reached up and took the lion's mane with his hand, and the three of us began to walk. We squeezed through the bedroom doorway down the hall, across the living room, and out the front door. We crossed the lawn, stopped out by the curb, turned, and looked back at the house.

It was nothing remarkable – a small white shotgun house, two bedrooms across the back, and a small kitchen to the left as we were facing it, a dining area and living room in the middle, an attached garage on the right. It still astounded me that something so unremarkable could store so much pain.

The three of us stood there for a long time looking at the house, Danny still holding my hand and the mane of the lion. Finally I saw him notice the bulldozer, sitting silently off to the right of the garage.

"Danny, that bulldozer is going to knock down the house. But he won't do it until you wave at him. That's his signal to start. Take your time to get ready. We're in no hurry." He stood and looked at the house for the longest time. Then he let go of my hand, waved at the bulldozer driver, and took my hand again.

With a rumble we could all feel through our feet, the powerful diesel cranked up. The driver pulled slowly up to the garage, levered his blade down and started crunching through at the corner. The roof of the garage caved in, and the driver backed out to let it fall. He moved over to the left of the porch and rammed directly into the living room, until it too began to fold up. He backed out, and then did the same at the left corner of the house. I heard screeching noises that I thought were the tiles on the kitchen counter folding in. The front half of the house buckled down.

The driver drove up on to the rubble in the middle, wood crunching under his tracks, until the weight of the dozer collapsed the pier and beam foundation, and the whole living room started to flatten. The house broke in the middle along the roofline, and the center portion of the house dropped, leaving exposed beams. He made a couple of more passes on the right, and then the left. We heard a terrible squeal when I suspected he ran over the old metal tub in the bathroom.

The driver backed up, pulled to the right of the house, and pushed on the back half of the house. He worked very methodically. He pushed through the back bedroom and it collapsed. He backed out, moved to the center, and smashed right through the back bedroom closet where all the pain had occurred. Little Danny's shoulders relaxed. One more pass, and Mamaw's bedroom collapsed.

All this time, the three of us stood and watched, fascinated and silent. The driver worked back and forth over the rubble of the house, breaking it up into smaller and smaller chunks. I had paid him well and told him to take his time. Finally the ruins were broken down and pulverized, and the only things left were the concrete steps at the front door, and another set of concrete steps to the kitchen.

The driver pulled over to the right of the house, lowered his blade to the ground, and pushed the rubble into the back yard. It took several passes for each section, but eventually he exposed raw dark dirt under the foundation, which hadn't seen light in many, many years.

At last it was done. The remains of the house were in the back yard, leaving only dirt where the house had stood. The driver backed out, turned off his engine. The silence felt good after all the noise and rumbling. Ticking sounds from the diesel engine were loud in the quiet.

The three of us stood there for a moment longer, then walked across the front lawn, up to the dirt, and stopped. I didn't want to go further, in case of random debris or nails. We just wanted to see, to confirm what had happened. Dark brown dirt, crisscrossed with bulldozer tracks, was all that remained. The house, the closet, and the place of bad memories – all was gone.

We stood and looked at the empty space for a long time. Then we turned, still holding on to one another, and walked away.

Epilogue

W as there more fear to be released? Of course there was. I had only recently realized how my child mind pictured an asylum – being put alone to die in the dark, in a small dungeon room like the scene from *Ben Hur*. That was the most horrific result of the abuse by Mamaw, but it wasn't something that was going to be healed overnight. The next several years was a repetition of what I've shared up to now – late nights of releasing the feelings, feeling the terror. I had to just hang on for the ride. Over time, I still had tremors, dreams, and periods of releasing the demons. But they were much less volatile, and shorter in duration. Gradually, the fears began to ease up and lose steam. I could once again go to bed at 11 PM, and sleep through the night, waking up refreshed in the morning.

Healing The Writer has been published, and I consider that a tremendous signal about the success of my healing journey. I don't try to say "I'm perfectly healed," or anything like that. What I say is, "I can heal the wounds, but I'll always have the scars." Will that old Mamaw energy leave vestiges that I will have to deal with? I strongly suspect so. It may be an ongoing process where I continue to weed out effects –

hopefully smaller and smaller – over time. The damage was just too horrific not to expect that to be the case. But all the evidence I can see also indicates my healing journey has been very successful. I am very content with how things have evolved.

CPSIA information can be obtained at www.ICGtesting.com
Printed in the USA
BVOW02s1640120216

436222BV00008B/11/P